WHAT EVER HAPPENED TO THE FAMILY?

WHAT EVER HAPPENED TO THE FAMILY?

A Psychologist Looks at Sixty Years of Change

Bobbie McKay

United Church Press
Cleveland

This book is printed on acid-free paper.

Library of Congress Cataloging-in-Publication Data

McKay, Bobbie, 1931–
What ever happened to the family? : a psychologist looks at sixty years of change / Bobbie McKay.
          p. cm.
Includes bibliographical references (p.   ).
ISBN 0-8298-0915-5 (acid-free paper)
1. Family—United States—History—20th century. 2. United States—Social conditions—1945– 1. Title.
          HQ535.M389   1992
          306.85'0973—dc20   91-34114
                    CIP

Printed in the United States of America.

10 9 8 7 6 5 4 3 2 1

United Church Press, 700 Prospect Avenue, East, Cleveland OH 44115-1100

To my mother, for her courage

*To my father, who believed I would
pay off the mortgages*

*And to Shannon, who is a special gift
and the first of the new generation*

CONTENTS

INTRODUCTION

Twenty-one years ago I began listening to families. As a clinical psychologist and also an ordained minister, I have been privileged to share in the lives of hundreds of families. Stories of their experiences have given me a depth of firsthand knowledge about families that transforms intellectual understanding into visible, undeniable reality. The seminars and workshops I've presented across the country underscored all the problems I was hearing in my office.

In the beginning, these families spoke to me of their fears and frustrations, their anger that life had become so unmanageable. As we came to know each other better, they began to share their disappointment and pain and the profound losses they were experiencing within the family. Their hopes and dreams of a shared, family future were being dashed on the hazardous rocks of uncontrollable change. The family was in jeopardy, assaulted on all sides by internal and external ruptures in a society that seemed to have lost its direction and focus.

Ruptures within the family were devastating. A rising divorce rate was wrenching families apart; single-parent and blended families were struggling to survive; extended-family ties were being broken; many parental roles were being filled by nonparental persons. Significant changes were occurring in the relationships between parents and children, focusing on issues of power and authority. Heated struggles and confrontations resulted in confusion over who was actually in charge of the family.

Ruptures outside the family had to do with powerful historical events and societal reactions that were putting direct pressure on the family. In sixty years we had experienced the economic disaster of the Great Depression; World War II, the Korean War, and the

Vietnam War; the societal explosions of the 1960s; Watergate and other governmental corruption; economic extremes of inflation, recession, and out-of-control credit; and the devastation of drug and alcohol abuse. Change was everywhere. Nothing seemed safe or reliable. These internal and external changes were highly reactive to each other, magnifying the chaos the family was experiencing.

Wherever I traveled the questions were always the same. What has happened to the family? How can children behave this way? Does anyone care anymore? What happened to rules and regulations? Where are respect and consideration for the rights of others? Is nothing sacred? Why is there so much anger and hate in the world? Can we restore some kind of order and meaning in our lives? When will these changes stop? Will the family survive?

The changes and challenges to family sanity were being felt in urban and rural America, in the inner city and the suburbs, on the West Coast and the East Coast and anyplace in between. Rich or poor, it didn't matter for no one was exempt. Change had taken over our lives and the family had lost its way.

In our struggles to deal with so many changes in the very core of our lives, we turned to a solution we hoped would relieve our pain and return our sanity. We became self-absorbed, looking for solace in the soothing sounds of narcissism. Opportunities were available everywhere to pursue our self-interests. "Do your own thing" became the rallying cry of people trying to feel better. But it was the worst solution we could have chosen. Our individual aggrandizement was highly injurious to the welfare of the family, and it rocked the moral underpinnings of our country. In fact, in the complex world in which we live, our survival depends on our capacity to work together. We can no longer live just for ourselves.

The scope of this book is to look at the changes of the last sixty years that have affected the family: what has happened, what we have learned, what the future holds. The book is not intended to be a sociological analysis of the family or a complete historical account of the last sixty years. Rather it is a picture of how we have struggled to deal with changes so profound they have altered our lives and penetrated the innermost parts of our souls.

A special friend recently told me, "We always remember the people we laugh with. But we never forget the people we cry with." The tears we have all shared in these years of struggle and change are unforgettable. But they bind us together and they proclaim a truth that must be heard.

This book was written to share those tears.

PART 1

WHAT HAPPENED

1

The Beginnings of Change:
The 1930s and 1940s

Immediately after World War I, if you had asked anyone what the family was, you would have received a fairly uniform answer. The family was still the traditional family that had characterized American society since its foundation. In the traditional family, the father was the head of the household, in theory if not always in fact; the mother was in a strong but secondary position; and the children were clearly subordinate to both parents. Members of the extended family often lived in the same household or close by. But today, one is hard pressed to find a family that fits this description. In fact, this family form may be rapidly approaching extinction. *What ever happened to the family?*

To answer this question we need to look back in history to see how the forces of societal change impinged upon the family in ways that significantly changed it. The first of these major disruptions occurred in the 1930s.

THE 1930s

In the 1930s the traditional family was shaken by the Great Depression, which put millions of people out of work. As it undermined the economy, it entered households, where it had devastating effects.

The economic depression caused a severe emotional depression, which took over the family. When the father lost his job, he began to lose some of the parental authority he had held for so long. Part of that authority was based on his ability to support the family financially. When that support was missing, the father's authority declined. If his unemployment continued into months or even years, it often caused an irreversible change in his personality. Hopeless, helpless, frustrated, angry, the father whom everyone had relied on felt like a failure to his family and to himself. One of my patients painfully remembered seeing her father sitting in a room illuminated by a bare light bulb, wearing an undershirt and pants, silently waiting for something to change. It was as if he had died, yet the corpse did not go away.

In some households, the mother tried to find ways to support the family. She looked for a paying job outside the home or did something at home to make money. In some working-class families, women had always worked outside the home. But these new efforts represented a major step toward the entrance of women into the paid work force. It was also the beginning of shared authority in the home. If the mother could produce some economic support, then she could begin to wield some of the authority in the family. But since she could not turn over any of her housekeeping or parenting responsibilities to the father (they were still *her* tasks), she was on her way to becoming the "super woman," who both cared for the family and worked to provide money for it.

The net result of these changes in parenting roles was the loss of significant care and support for the children in the family. In a crisis of this magnitude, children needed the reassurance that their parents would continue to provide for their needs. As their world was crumbling around them, children needed to know that stability still existed in the family. But many parents were physically and emotionally unable to provide this reassurance or stability. Children were expected to help—to earn money if possible and to stay out of the way of the strained situations at home. To survive, they learned to work hard, be invisible, keep silent, and feel afraid.

The result of the Depression was years of turmoil, fear, and pain. Some people have never recovered from it. The economic collapse of the 1930s still haunts them, creating sleepless nights and anxious moments whenever some change seems to threaten the safety of their world. Many people in their fifties today are still suffering from their experiences as children growing up during the Depression. Their insecurity expresses itself as a kind of passivity or panic in the face of what they perceive as hopelessness and helplessness. In particular it is their invisibility and fear that have made it difficult for them to speak out on issues affecting their lives within the family and in the community as well.

The Depression taught us many profound lessons:

▷ Promises can be broken.
▷ Families can be destroyed.
▷ Individuals can be permanently damaged by circumstances beyond their control.
▷ The government cannot guarantee protection from economic disaster.
▷ The American democratic system cannot fulfill the dream of a good life for everyone.

Within the family, we learned parallel truths:

▷ Father could lose his power.
▷ Mother could become a breadwinner and therefore less available as a nurturer.
▷ Parental authority, previously so well defined and understood, could fall apart or be unavailable.

No wonder the children of the Depression were so afraid. In silence, they adapted. But they did not forget.

THE 1940s

In the 1940s another explosion outside the family deeply affected family life—World War II. It was a terrible time of great losses. Husbands, sons, and some daughters left home to fight in the war effort. Almost every family had someone involved. Some never returned to the family. Others returned broken and damaged. Parents lost children, and children lost parents and siblings and members of the extended family.

But paradoxically, the war energized us; it mobilized us. It took us out of the desperation of the Depression and put us into a time of record employment. A growing economy brought renewed excitement and a sense of possibility. We came together as a nation determined to defeat our treacherous enemies and win this war for freedom.

Anyone who watches World War II movies can see how well defined our roles became: Men were truly men, brave and strong. Women were truly women, courageous and confident. Children were proud and loyal. Americans were filled with the spirit that had brought this country into being. We were revitalized and reconnected to our heritage. We were strong; we were tough; we felt wonderful because we were so filled with pride for our country and for our war effort. We ate Spam without grumbling too much. We gave up nylon stockings and gasoline and felt proud rather than deprived. We learned about places and people all around the world that we had never known before. We were unified, not fragmented as we are today. Whatever trials and tribulations we had suffered in the preceding decade were forgotten as we mobilized around the cause of world freedom.

The unavailability of parents away in the military or at war work meant the growing independence of children. The impact of this independence may be seen as the children born in the war years of the 1940s became the outspoken adolescent and adult rebels of the 1960s. Their experience marked them indelibly with a belief in the importance of freedom and the power of the community gathered to change society. As their parents had devoted their very lives to the cause of political freedom, so the children born in the war years would devote part of their adult lives to the causes of peace and personal freedom. Their adherence to their own causes, which exploded in the 1960s, was no less zealous than that of their parents to the war in the 1940s.

Many of the women who entered the work force in the war were given high levels of responsibility, and they did their jobs efficiently and competently. No wonder their daughters were so ready for the women's liberation movement of the 1960s. Rosie the riveter, that powerful symbol of women working side by side with men in war factories, produced daughters who were ready for the experience of their own power and authority. Like their mothers before them, these daughters, born in the 1940s and reaching adolescence and young adulthood in the 1960s, were more than ready to fight for equal participation and equal status. Rosie was an effective model! Her daughters would never again accept second-class citizenship and less-than-equal rights. Rosie's granddaughters, entering their own adolescence and adulthood in the 1980s, further reflected this change. They would became part of a growing number of young women choosing to start their careers before having children or simply not having children at all.

In spite of the losses we suffered as a nation, as families, and as individuals, the 1940s remain a time of great pride and curious peacefulness. Life was simpler and more manageable because everyone was involved in the war effort. There were few distractions. There was no gas for travel, and few consumer goods to purchase. Television hadn't been invented. The family turned to itself and the neighborhood for strength and support. Teenagers did not rebel; marriages tended to remain intact and permanent; minor family problems were greatly overshadowed by the job that needed to be done. Crime rates were low; savings were up. We dreamed only of the time when victory would be ours, wars would end, and all would be well. When peace finally came, the future seemed almost engorged with possibilities.

How ill prepared we were when the Korean war began in the summer of 1949. We were painfully back to a place we never wanted to face again. Peace was over.

2

The Calm Before the Storm: The 1950s

The Korean War began as a skirmish in 1949 and within six months had developed into a full-scale war. Because it came so close on the heels of World War II, we were devastated and unprepared. It seemed too much to endure. We were eager to live normal lives and were very confused about this new conflict, which was frequently called a police action, a description that made little sense in the light of the casualties we suffered. When the war ended in July 1953, we believed that peace was finally ours. Surely wars were ended for all time, and families could be together at last.

As we shifted into a peacetime economy, we became a mobile society. Gasoline became available for travel. At the same time, expanding industry required many of its employees to travel or even relocate. Executive moves became part of many young professionals' path to success. We traveled to enrich our lives, to see parts of the United States we'd never seen. We traveled because it was new and exciting and we wanted to test our horizons. We still believed in the pioneer spirit, which urged us to see new places and explore new possibilities. The boundaries of our families, neighborhoods, and local communities no longer contained us.

THE NUCLEAR FAMILY AND PERMISSIVENESS

In all new experiences and change, there is always a price to pay. The price we paid for our expansiveness in the 1950s was the loss of the extended family. As we broke new ground, we left behind old supports and structures that had sustained and supported us. As we looked ahead with excitement and hope, we separated ourselves from the traditional family model that had supported us for many years. We left extended family and familiar neighborhoods and communities and entered a brave new world of family life called the nuclear family. We became a nucleus consisting only of dad, mom, and the kids. We were not only a family on the move, we were a family on our own.

Having grown up in the Depression and suffered the pain and loss of World War II, now as parents in the postwar era, we wanted to be free of fear and struggle. We wanted life to be good for everyone, and we were determined that our children would have everything just right. We wanted them to have a life that was peaceful, loving, and filled with the warmth of being together.

Because so many of us could no longer draw on the accumulated experience and wisdom of the extended family to guide us in this new territory of the nuclear family, it's no wonder that we fell in love with psychology. Psychology seemed to have all the answers to creating the happy, well-adjusted family we longed for. We read books about child rearing and talked endlessly about how to do it just right. We wanted to change what our parents had done *to* us by what we would do *for* our children. It was not that our parents had not loved us or had treated us badly. It was rather that we would love our children *properly*, treat them with great respect, and arrange their lives so that there would be no stress and minimal trouble. We thought we could avoid family conflict and unhappiness if we used our new understandings of human development and behavior.

We began to experiment in the family. Parental authority became more shared, with mom and dad *both* in charge. We extended democracy to the children, as we began to give them some authority. In our desire to please them, it was inevitable that we should embrace permissiveness with our whole mind and heart. Permissiveness, as we saw it, allowed us to be friends to our children and thereby somewhat invisible as parents. If we did not have to be the visible authority in the family, the traditional parental role, then surely our children would not have to struggle with us. Instead, they would always love us in return for the specialness of our care, and our fears of loss and conflict would be assuaged. It would be a long time before we would understand that love alone, without parental discipline, is not enough.

The problem was that as parents became friends to their children, the boundaries between children and parents became less well defined and thereby more confusing. The net result was the beginning of no parenting, and the seeds for future chaotic family relationships began to take root.

TELEVISION

As peace became a reality, all kinds of consumer goods began to flood the market, and we had the savings, accumulated during the war years, to buy those goods. We could purchase the goods that would support the family life we believed we could finally achieve. Television was able to splice all the pieces together. Television showed us what consumer products to buy and how good we would feel if we bought them. It captured our imagination and our wallet. We loved it and watched it with increasing fascination and frequency. It was our special toy and we were absolutely ready for it. The family that had long awaited the time when it could be reunited was fully involved in the process of being together. We were the family that would stay together, play together, and pray together. We built white picket fences around our houses to ensure our togetherness, and we turned on the television at night to watch our programs.

The children born during the Depression were the parents of the children born in the 1950s. Their own "inner child" was alive and well and determined that this new generation of children born in the post-Depression and postwar era would live lives that were safe and reliable, without trouble or conflict, protected by the experience of being together.

As we'd gathered around the radio to listen to our programs as a family, we now congregated in front of the television to learn all about the family. We watched entranced as "Father Knows Best," "Leave It to Beaver," and "I Love Lucy" paraded family life before our eyes. Here was the family we longed to experience, full of shared humor, togetherness, warmth, love, and simplicity. Whatever conflicts appeared in that wonderful entertainment box were clearly resolved by the end of the program. We now had visible models of family life, and because the actors appeared to be "real people," the same kinds of lives seemed almost within our grasp. Even if we understood we were just seeing a story, the experience seemed entirely real. Because it happened to us night after night, year after year, we gradually became seduced by the story. We entered the unreality of television because it matched our needs.

Clearly we had no idea then of the price we would have to pay for our delusion. Our benign toy would utterly change our lives, dilute our intimate relationships, and ultimately try to convince us that fantasy was truth. But we bought the distortion and the whole picture of fictionalized family life it portrayed. It seemed so simple—at least it looked so simple—on television.

3

Major Convulsions: The 1960s

But unreality can last only so long. Predictably, the pleasant fantasies of the 1950s were followed by the painful reality of the 1960s. Family togetherness was exploded by a series of convulsions, both in our families and in the society around us, that changed our lives. Everywhere we looked, some major force was destroying the safe and comfortable life we had so carefully arranged in the preceding decade. The calm we had experienced then was like the eye of the hurricane. The storm was surrounding us and gathering strength. Nothing could stop or contain it.

SOCIETAL EXPLOSIONS

The explosions began with the civil rights movement, which visibly demonstrated the continuing prejudice and hostility toward blacks in this country. We had to face the fact that the Civil War had not ended cruelty to blacks. We were a nation that preached acceptance of blacks and practiced humiliation of them. We played lip service to equality and turned away from any action that promised actual, equal rights to life, liberty, and the pursuit of happiness. We were a nation divided, though we proclaimed a liberal stance toward integration and unification.

The education of black children became an issue that had to be addressed. Segregated not only in their present life but also from the possibility of any kind of equal economic future, they were in a situation that was particularly shameful in a country that promised equal opportunity for all. If we could not agree on the education of black children, how were we ever going to deal with the prejudice that existed against most black adults?

The convulsions continued with the women's liberation movement, which revealed the blatant double standard that existed between women and men, according to which women were treated as second-class citizens, with minimal rights and few expectations that anything would be different in the future. As women struggled to voice their concerns, the injustice of their situation became more exposed. Women were being kept out of some professions and occupations and were paid less than men in all fields of work. The courage and protests of those women who tried to point out the need for change were generally met with violent, reactive power plays to keep women "in their place." Although in a kind of token liberalism, some women were accepted in lower management positions, their "place" remained the same, one down from the top.

The women's movement became even more explosive as "sisters" turned against "sisters," for not every woman wanted to be "liberated." Where women should have been unified they were painfully at odds. As the movement became more complex, it grew into a tidal wave that challenged men and women to look at more fundamental questions of human rights and liberation. As in the civil rights movement, equality for all could be verbalized but was not demonstrated.

At the same time, the sexual revolution burst upon our lives, tearing apart our safe, well-defined sexual attitudes and behaviors, making all too visible that which we'd thought was private and personal. Television, movies, and other media or art forms eroded the sexual barriers we'd lived with for so long. Everywhere we looked we could see intimate details of people engaging in various sexual practices. We decided that being "healthy" meant eliminating sexual inhibitions. We were determined to become free of the barriers and interferences with our sexual pleasures. We became a nation obsessed with sexuality.

We didn't anticipate the excesses to which the media would go to meet our demands for sexual freedom. They responded to our voyeuristic insistence on seeing and hearing all and provided continuous opportunities for us to experience sexual freedom. The irony, as we know it today, is that all this sexual freedom has produced an epidemic of sexual apathy and indifference.

We needed substance and direction, but psychology was just in its infancy and couldn't provide the help we needed. So a kind of popular psychology emerged as the human-potential movement, which attempted to deal with our overwhelming need for help. New schemes and systems were developed to deal with our pain. A variety of therapeutic words became part of our everyday vocabulary. We worked hard to gain control in a world that felt increasingly chaotic and out of control. But manipulative and greedy people also got into the act, taking advantage of our pain and leading us down inappropriate and unhealthy paths. They promised us relief: a quick fix or a weekend cure. But it was like putting a Band-Aid on a broken artery. Our pain and vulnerability were simply too complex to respond to a fast-food kind of cure. We looked for any resource that would promise us a way out of our despair. The resources multiplied, but our powers of discrimination decreased.

Overshadowing these domestic convulsions was the Vietnam War. Official United States involvement began in March 1965, when President Lyndon Johnson sent the marines into action. Once again Americans were caught up in a war across the world in a place most of us hardly knew existed. It was too much, too soon. As the war dragged on and casualties mounted, national opinion was deeply divided on whether the country should be fighting in Southeast Asia at all.

THE FRACTURED FAMILY

While society was exploding around us, the family was suffering from its own internal convulsions. We were no longer the safe, well-ordered, stay-together nuclear family of the 1950s. In less than a decade our world had turned upside down. We became the fractured family, fractured so severely that in the 1990s we have not yet recovered. In biblical terms, members turned against each other: son against father, daughter against mother, husband against wife. Enmity expanded to set neighbor against neighbor, individual against society, citizen against the government. Rebellion was the rule, and no tenet was so sacred that it could not be rebelled against.

This rebellion began with our adolescent children. Suddenly, or so it seemed, they were questioning our beliefs, our values, and what remained of the authority structure in the family by demanding to be heard and insisting on being different from us. Their rejection of the tidy picture of life we'd created was symbolized by their long hair and loud music. The long hair defied conventional pictures of what "proper" young women and men should look like. The loud music drowned out our protests, increased our separateness, and cut off communication between us. The closeness we parents had lovingly cultivated in the 1950s was shattered by the amplification of sound that was harsh, piercing, and chaotic. We couldn't stand it, which meant our protesting children clung to it to maintain their difference from us. Later in the 1960s our children's loud music became associated with the consumption of drugs and alcohol. Rock concerts became meccas for drug dealers and drug takers. The intensity of the music was magnified by the drug-induced, internal chaos of the audience.

Our children became the "flower children," exposed to the horror of the Vietnam War and our confused efforts to deal with it. Having been born in the 1940s, they had already seen our courage, determination, and devotion to a cause in World War II. Now they had their own cause. What rallied them in one massive outcry was their demands for peace and freedom. Peace meant the end of the Vietnam War, and they worked incessantly to bring that about. But freedom was a far more complicated issue than just bringing the war to an end.

The freedom our children sought was not only from conscription but also from societal rules and regulations that parents and other authorities imposed. Alongside the Vietnam War a smaller war had begun between the forces of the "old," represented by parental and societal authority, and forces of the "new," represented by a new generation of adolescents and postadolescents (including some elderly "adolescents" in their forties). This war was being fought in homes, schools, and communities, wherever this new generation felt inhibited by our rules and regulations.

Defiance became a way of life. "You can't make me" became the rallying words of rebellion. This new generational war, which is still going on, was fought with weapons of verbal abuse and physical defiance. As parents we weren't able to create a peaceful coexistence between young and old. We couldn't find a solution in which both sides could experience a sense of winning. Instead, authority structures everywhere crumbled and surrendered. Parents finally had had it. We had no energy left to continue the battle. We had been overwhelmed by all the revolutionary changes and had given up. We'd done our best, but it was clearly not good enough. We had no more solutions to ease the pain of too many changes in too many places.

We rationalized our surrender by saying that our children were pretty smart; we conceded that rules could become unimportant and archaic; we temporized that perhaps it was all just a passing whim, and the "kids" would eventually grow up. We tried to convince ourselves that our children really did know what was best. We gave them credit for knowledge and understanding that can only come with age and experience.

Our passive surrender in the face of this adolescent rebellion was the worst response we could give. Our children needed a parental and societal response that would stand firm while they, as was appropriate to the young, challenged it with demands for change. Our children needed to know that certain values and beliefs were solidly entrenched in our societal fabric.

Instead, we showed them that they had little to rely on except themselves. As we had separated from our own extended families in the mobile society of the 1950s, they began to break away from us and all we valued, turning the nuclear family into the fractured family. We had taught them to be independent, and they were. Now we were teaching them there were no rules, no solid ground on which to stand except that of their own making and choosing. The stage was set for chaos.

DRUGS

Chaos arrived in the form of drugs. If there was one single factor that changed family life in America, it was the availability of drugs, which became widespread in the 1960s. As we failed to set limits and controls, our children learned that drugs could send them entirely beyond our reach. They had found the way both to defy us and to be utterly different from us. Whereas we were conservative, powerless, and "square," they were liberal, powerful, and willing to risk their lives with substances that could literally kill them.

American society is still reeling under the catastrophic impact of drugs. Drugs have changed the personality of our children, caused heartbreak and disaster, and destroyed families. They have supported the sexual revolution, causing children to have sexual experiences long before they were socially and emotionally mature enough to handle them. They have produced a sexual morality that says, "Anything goes with anyone." Multiple partners meant the increase of sexually transmitted diseases. Love and fidelity were lost in the murky haze of drugs, alcohol, and promiscuity.

Drugs created a world of anger and aggressiveness in the midst of a cry for peace. Our children were drowning their sorrows and problems in substances that were killing their chances to live. Families were wrenched apart by children who could no longer contain their anger either toward other family members or toward themselves.

Some adolescents and young adults began to opt out of conventional society, moving into communal living situations that often turned out to be wretched, filthy, inhuman places of mere existence, not living. Their surroundings represented a violent protest against the values of order and cleanliness that they saw around them. The drugs they took allowed them to be blind to their surroundings and deaf to any voice of reason or hope. They were the lost ones for whom life no longer had meaning. Contaminated by what they ingested or forced into their bodies, many of them lost touch with reality and began to die. For other young people, drugs meant actual suicide attempts, repeated until they successfully accomplished their desire to be rid of the problem of living.

As parents, we didn't realize to what extent our children were becoming physically addicted to drugs and alcohol. We didn't know about dual addictions. We couldn't see how dangerous the situation had become. All we knew was that we'd lost the ability to be in charge. Our children were now treating us in ways we would never have treated our parents. Each new confrontation became a nightmare. We thought it couldn't get worse. *But we were wrong.*

4

Continuing Convulsions: The 1970s

In the 1970s an even more alarming breakdown in authority occurred. As a result of the Watergate scandal, United States President Richard Nixon resigned from office, after he had been charged with attempting to cover up criminal government activities. Honesty and truth no longer existed at the highest level of authority. Our government, clearly a powerful, symbolic parent, was seen to be corrupt. The keepers of the laws and rules of society were not there for its members. Many Americans were shocked that this nation, begun with such high ideals and careful planning, could have sunk to this level of deception and dishonesty. Our national family was deeply troubled, even as our personal families were.

THE CHILD-DOMINATED FAMILY AND THE SINGLE-PARENT FAMILY

In keeping with increasing social changes all around us, the fractured families of the 1960s divided into two new forms of family life: the child-dominated family and the single-parent family.

The child-dominated family was the inevitable result of the loss of parental authority in the home. As parents gave up being parents, children stepped into fill the void. But these were not the adolescents

who had rocked their parents' lives in the 1960s. These were younger
children, who had become infected with the same antisocial virus.
Aggressive, angry, unparented children began to dominate the
household. They literally ran the family ragged. Their needs and
desires became the focal point of the family. Even very young
children exhibited provocative behavior. They manipulated the family with temper tantrums, wildly emotional scenes, and actions that
were out of control. No one said no to them because no one wanted
the responsibility of being a parent.

Child-dominated families are not happy families. Children really
don't want to run the family; they do it only out of desperation when
their own needs are not being met. They need us to be steady,
consistent, and in control of their world. They need us to be parents.
When they don't get what they need from us, they show us their
confusion and desperation. By putting pressure on us, their unconscious hope is we'll come to our senses and become parents again.

Parents in the 1950s had listened to the voice of psychology, which
had told them to be careful in rearing their children, to pay attention
to their development, and to learn to be good parents. It had also
reminded them of the importance of the early years in the formation
of personality and character. We had anxiously tried to be really
good parents, watching out for our children's psychological growth
like hawks circling around a rabbit, looking for signs that we weren't
doing it right. We wanted them to feel good about themselves. We
wanted them to have a wonderful childhood. We thought the way to
accomplish that was to fill their lives with all the good things and
good times we could provide. But we and our children were like
ships that pass in the night, missing each other at every turn.

We had provided our children with what *we* wanted for them, not
what *they* needed. Their attempt to dominate the family was their
way of trying to get the family back on track. It was as if they were
saying to us, "If I show you how out of control I can be, then will
you give me what I need?" We thought their efforts at domination
meant they weren't happy, so we tried even harder to make our
dreams of a happy childhood come true. We were all innocent
victims of a culture gone crazy on popular psychology.

The permissiveness of the 1950s had become the desperation of
the 1960s, which gave way to the hopelessness of the 1970s. We had
taken the voice of psychology and pushed it through a pastry tube of
pop psychology, which extruded a product that bore little resem-

blance to the original formulation. All parental power seemed to be smothered under a blanket of fear lest we "raise our children wrong" or do something to cause them a lifetime of suffering. As children seized control and were clearly no happier, we began to give up parenting. We were particularly stunned by the number of mothers choosing to leave home, husbands, and children because they couldn't tolerate the pain any longer.

At the same time a rising divorce rate was creating a growing number of single-parent families. As the number of divorces increased, we saw more deeply the sadness and loss that was afflicting the American family. We were not staying or playing together because we were enmeshed in marital and familial disharmony. We were not praying together because our spiritual and religious values seemed to be lost and overwhelmed by the chaos in our lives. Our dream of togetherness was gone.

THE DECLINE OF THE CHURCH AND THE SCHOOL

Our losses continued to mount as the church, which had been a stable influence for morality in the community, began to decline. Church attendance was down; churches were closing; youth programs were being eliminated because of increasing costs. Church-related groups such as the Scouts, the YWCA, and the YMCA, were scaled down as costs rose and funds were short. Our attitude toward the church as a pivotal force in our lives was also changing. The church was regarded by many people primarily as a social group where they could meet new friends and attend various lectures and other programs. Church was where we took our children for religious education, but it was not a visible catalyst for redemption, nor did it seem to have significant influence on changing our lives.

As children move out of the family toward adulthood and independence in the outside world, they need a powerful ally outside the family to make the journey less hazardous. The church and church-related groups are visible beacons on the "other side." At their peak, they provided our children with a necessary bridge to adulthood. Without such extra-familial support systems, children are forced to discover their own resources to help survive the journey to maturity. Unfortunately for some children, the resources they turned to often had no moral underpinnings, leaving them mired in an underworld of antisocial behavior and drugs.

The final institution to fall, after the government, the family, and the church, was the school. The deterioration of the public school system was the final blow in a series of unendurable losses to the family. Parents had believed they could always count on the schools to educate their children. If all else failed, at least our children would learn how to survive in the world through the path of knowledge. We had hoped that the chaos in the family and society that had begun in the 1960s and increased in the 1970s hadn't infected our educational system as well. But we were wrong. Our schools were also caught in the onslaught of change, and their decline was no different from the decline in other institutions.

In the 1970s the schools were struggling under pressures of racial integration and the discovery that many students were not receiving the kind of education they needed to become good citizens. Americans had had a sense of national pride in their educational system, believing it was the best in the world. As we entered the space age, we believed we could provide such an enriched curriculum in science and math that we would continue to dominate the world with our Yankee genius.

What a shock to discover that our children were not being educated. As the schools "enriched" their curriculum by bringing psychology into the classroom, teachers were burdened with the double responsibility of being both teachers and therapists. No longer simply concerned whether Johnny learned to read or multiply, Johnny's teacher also had to worry about Johnny's self-esteem and ego development. It was a responsibility that should never have been allowed to enter the classroom.

Teachers not only became personal therapists to their students, they had to take on parental roles as well. But as they struggled under that triple load, the teaching function became shortchanged. The more time was spent in shoring up defective egos, or maintaining discipline, the less time was available to satisfy a child's hunger for knowledge.

By this time, what had begun in the home was now happening in the school. The classroom had become an extension of the home environment. Well-meaning educators were not providing what every child must have: information, discipline, structure, safety, consistency, love, and respect. It was clearly a situation of good intentions gone awry: parents and teachers were trying hard to provide what they thought the young needed; children and adolescents were screaming for some structure to provide them with safety. As the situation became more chaotic, children increasingly engaged in negative behaviors, demanding any attention adults would give them.

As teachers lost control of classrooms, the potential for learning diminished even further. Respect for the school and the teaching staff became a thing of the past. No longer was a teacher exempt from that well-worn challenge: "You can't make me!" Every defiant behavior that was tolerated became a model and excuse for more antisocial behavior. Teachers were being tested on a moment-by-moment basis. Any failure to pass the test became a signal to the students that the enemy was weakening. It became a war between the children and the authorities.

The war was lost over the issue of drugs in the schools. When drugs appeared, the students lost their ability to learn. Drugs were available in classrooms, corridors, bathrooms, playgrounds, or just outside school property. Anytime a student wanted anything he or she could have it, for money or whatever else he or she wanted to "put up." That could mean sexual favors as well as items stolen from home to pay for the drugs. When students couldn't afford drugs, they could always steal some "booze" from their parents to tide them over until they could get their next drug fix.

It's no wonder good teachers began to leave the field. Teachers had become prisoners in the same way parents were. They could earn far greater salaries (for far less trouble) in another profession. There was little reason for them to stay because the necessary environment for teaching was gone. As they left, the educational system slipped to a new low.

NARCISSISM

To make matters worse, we were in the midst of an economic crisis in the 1970s. The economy seemed chaotic; inflation was rapidly increasing. We were becoming aware that the nation was dividing itself into those who could afford to live and those who could not. The poor became visible and audible. Watergate had taught us what happens when an institution becomes so large and complex it cannot police itself. How much worse was it going to get?

Everywhere we looked, the American dream seemed to be dying. Our cities were full of violence. Our homes were fraught with conflict and disillusion. Our schools were crumbling, and our churches were dying. We had lost hope.

No wonder we were so ripe for a way of life that looked as if it would save us all. Narcissism entered our lives during the 1970s. The tenets of narcissism were these: You are indeed the most important person in your life; you deserve to have the best; you need to look out only for yourself. You must get all you want; take what you need; do what will make you happy. You are it!

To eyes tired of seeing all the chaos, to ears tired of hearing how difficult everything was, to hearts heavy with the pain and sorrow of dreams that were dead, the message of narcissism offered a new hope and a new way.

We bought narcissism. We lived it, breathed it, tried to convert others to it. Once again, we knew how to live. The dream was back and we would survive. This new aspect of popular psychology was our new religion, an opiate that would remove our pain and heal us. We became addicted to the message, and like all good addicts, we always found the time and money to obtain what we needed: an orgasmic moment, an intense weekend experience, a guru to show us the way to nirvana.

Groups emerged everywhere to glorify the self; quantities of books appeared offering ways to improve the self. We elevated the self to incredible heights, constantly looking for new resources and people to provide a "quick fix" for our new obsession. Gurus gained national reputations as guardians of the self.

Our obsession with the self was fueled by the plethora of consumer goods and easy availability of credit cards. These enabled us to live life on our demand. We could have what we wanted when we wanted it. We didn't have to curb our impulses, restrict our purchases, or delay gratifying our wishes until we could afford them. All we had to do was follow the yellow brick road of "if you want it, get it."

But the heights of self-obsesssion and self-gratification only led to deep caverns of despair. The reality was that everything was worse rather than better. The message of narcissism was empty, although it continues to be a siren song for many even today. As it single-mindedly concentrated on the self, telling us we were our own best friends, self-sufficient individuals who did not need anyone else, it separated us even further from one another. The alienation we felt in our families and marriages became magnified and increased by the medicine of narcissism.

In having it all for ourselves, we had nothing. This time we did not approach the new decade of the 1980s hoping for something different. It was as if we were suspended in time, waiting for the next blow to fall. And it did.

5

No Relief in Sight: The 1980s

We were less innocent when the 1980s began. We'd already been through two decades of turmoil and knew the struggle was not over. We had begun to recognize that although we had apparently finished with the horror and destruction of the Vietnam War, we were into something else that wasn't called a war but had many of the ingredients of a revolution.

REVOLUTION, VIOLENCE, AND DRUGS

We were bombarded by change—changes in the rules and values and attitudes of society outside the family and changes in our relationships within the family. We were wounded by confrontations and ruptures in the family, ugly scenes in which everyone was the loser. Under the banner of narcissism we were all fair game for anyone who wanted to have his or her own way and express aggression or other antisocial feelings. Obscene words and gestures became the norm. "Let it all hang out" was the rationalization. We were all the victims of this new model of social interaction.

We were stunned by the increasing violence in the home and in society. It came in many forms: the violence of ugly words, which became commonplace in our language; the violence of hostility as crime increased; the violence and horror of children damaged by physical and sexual abuse; the violence of women beaten and injured in the home.

No family was exempt from this revolution; no family was safe, although some rode it out better than others. It reached rich and poor, powerful and helpless. Like an enemy who has occupied the land, the revolution surrounded us, captured us, and took us prisoner.

The most powerful weapon of this revolution was drugs. Drugs, which had begun in the 1960s and grew to uncontrollable proportions in the 1980s, sustained the revolution, accounted for its fury, and fueled the flame of its hostility. Drugs were all the more dangerous because they were viewed as desirable rather than threatening. No one could begin to estimate what the toll on family life in America would be as a result of the entrance of drugs into our society.

Drugs changed everything from our most intimate relationships to the stability of the government. They changed people's morals, attitudes, behaviors, emotions, and ability to discriminate and judge. They drowned out the voice of conscience and caused people to act in immoral and illegal ways; they helped create an amoral society.

Drugs ruptured family life. Adolescents on drugs engaged in countless scenes of destructive behavior; drugs killed our children outright or caused them to attempt suicide, as noted previously. Even their "casual" use destroyed growth, and their use during pregnancy often produced newborns who were also addicts or otherwise damaged.

Alcohol was already being abused by many adolescents and adults. If alcohol and drugs alone weren't enough, many people decided to combine them to attain a really "great high." Husbands and wives who were abusers of alcohol or drugs or both fought battles of drugged idiocy with no meaning and no resolution. They lost jobs and spent money recklessly and foolishly. Violence erupted on countless occasions with a terrifying randomness. Young children suffered exposure to emotions far in excess of what they could comprehend or tolerate.

As we became more sophisticated in making and taking drugs, the danger increased. Dual addictions are now commonplace. Many Americans seem bent on mass suicide through the consumption of toxic substances that will injure and finally kill them.

In single-parent families the cost was too great. One parent simply couldn't handle what was happening. An adolescent on drugs, a younger child with emotional problems, a spouse not making child-care payments—any of these was enough to cause the collapse of the family. No one was taking care of anyone. In child-dominated families, the end of parenting had already begun. Any single crisis could send the family over the edge, because there was no anchoring parent to hold the family together. It was understandable that two new extreme forms of family emerged to try to deal with the problem: the couple family and the blended family, both of which continue today.

THE COUPLE FAMILY

The couple family consisted of two adults who consciously decided not to have children. What better solution to the problem of parenting than to avoid it. People looked around at families in constant crisis and said, "We don't need this." The columnist Ann Landers is said to have asked a question of her readers: "Knowing what you do now, would you still choose to have children?" And the answer was reported to have been an overwhelming no!

Whether or not one can put stock in an informal inquiry through a newspaper column, the question was being answered by the increasing number of couples who were choosing not to have children. Unfortunately those couples were also indirectly supporting the narcissism of the 1970s, which admonished us to be self-absorbed as well as self-contained. We can ill afford to solve our problems by cutting off the future. Creating families, caring for the young, and teaching future generations are all part of our social and biological heritage. We will change the very core of our society if we eliminate that experience.

THE BLENDED FAMILY

In the blended family, courageous parents took on many children, those of the former family of each spouse as well as those they might have together. The blended family tried to solve the problem of the single-parent family by combining forces and producing two parents. The difficulty, of course, was the enormity of the task. If it was hard to look after three children from one family, imagine what it was like with six children from two families! The naive hope that we could combine previous families in a new family configuration and salvage family life was all too often dashed on the reality of too many children, too little money, too many stresses, too little time, and too much residue from the past family experience brought into the new family.

The divorce rate among remarried couples climbed to new heights. Two of every three remarriages failed, a fact that caused new waves of grief and loss to every member of the family. It was simply too hard. We thought we'd heal in the remarriage, and instead we discovered new hurts. We thought the children would benefit from a broader family experience, and instead we found eruptions of sibling rivalry and hate. We thought our love would carry us through the hard times, and we found ourselves resenting the lack of money and the constant pressure to provide it. We couldn't change the present, let alone deal with the pain of past family experiences. Our hopes and dreams were dashed on the reality of a load that felt too heavy to carry. The fantasy we watched on television depicting the joys of blended-family life turned out to be a nightmare we lived each day.

If these blended families were to succeed, they would do it with hard and continuous work, not with playful frivolity of the "Brady Bunch." The problem with the blended family was that we didn't know how long to work on it or when to give up. Only now are we understanding that it takes five to seven years to bring a blended family through the inevitable chaos that surrounds the beginning of this new family structure. Any shorter time doesn't allow for all the dynamics of change that are involved. When two divorced (or widowed) people who already have children marry, all the unfinished issues of the old families are brought into the new family structure, where they are caught up and rerun in their entirety. It is years before problems are resolved.

That blended families are here to stay is reflected in the prediction, by the Step Family Association of America, that by the year 2000, they will be the most common form of family life in America. They are the natural result of a rising divorce rate *and* our continued determination to marry and raise families.

PREADOLESCENT VIOLENCE

As we saw changes in family configurations during the 1980s, we also experienced increasing turbulence among our preadolescent population. Our ten-, eleven-, and twelve-year-olds were showing behavioral changes similar to those that we had seen in teenagers in the preceding decades. These preadolescents, like their older siblings, were also experimenting with drugs and alcohol prematurely and discovering social and sexual awareness.

The most serious problem we were finding with these preadolescents was their propensity toward violence. They were becoming increasingly violent in their peer relationships, especially to children they perceived as different from themselves. They were becoming verbally abusive to adults they didn't like or who "interfered" with their activities. They were becoming physically violent with property both in schools and neighborhoods.

These children who behaved in violent, abusive ways were not underprivileged children living in poverty. These were children of affluent parents fast forwarding into a destructive adolescence. Once again, their behavior called out for someone to stop them. But worn-out parents were hard pressed even to begin to know what to do with this group. They turned to the school for solutions, but the school had its hands full trying to cope with the same hostility and disrespect in the classroom. This was a brand new problem for all of us.

ADOLESCENT SUICIDE

As preteens moved into violence, more and more adolescents moved on to suicide. The suicide rate among adolescents began to climb. Adults were horrified to find out how many young people didn't want to live any more. Single suicides became the signal for multiple suicides and copy-cat suicide attempts in various parts of the country. It was as if suicide were contagious. For many adolescents, suicide attempts were an anguished cry for help. For an undetermined number, suicide attempts and actual suicides were probably the result of drugs or alcohol abuse or both. For a few, the threat of suicide was the blackmail they used to obtain what they wanted from adults.

We parents were terrified that it might happen in our family. It was the worst experience we could imagine. We were afraid to put any pressure on our offspring lest we ourselves do something that would result in our child's choosing to die. We believed that if that happened, we would not be able to survive.

No one seemed to know what to do about these changes in the

family or where they would take us. Even the experts seemed divided
in their opinions about child rearing. No one could reassure us that
some catastrophe wouldn't happen to our family.

THE PERPETUAL FAMILY

As we struggled just to survive, we encountered yet another new
phenomenon in family life. Our young adult population, the children
we thought were finally grown up and ready to go out on their own,
began to return home to stay, and stay, and stay. They came back
from college graduations to stay at home. They came back from
failed marriages to stay at home. They came back from jobs that
hadn't worked out to stay at home. What was especially dismaying
was that these were the children who couldn't wait to leave home,
the children who had railed against our traditions and expectations.
The reasons they gave for returning were economic: It's too expensive out there. We can't make it out there. We can't afford to furnish
an apartment. We'll leave as soon as we . . . But they did not leave.
It began to look as if a new family form had begun called the
perpetual family.

REJECTED AND ABUSED CHILDREN

The 1980s produced a new way to handle stressful parent-child
relationships: get rid of them; throw the children out. As we became
a society that created disposable products, so we became a society
that disposed of our children when the going got too rough. In 1985
an article in the St. Louis Post Dispatch, "Lost Children and Run-
aways," estimated that more than 1 million American children had
left home to try to make it on their own. These were described as
children from white, middle-class, and upper-middle-class families,
whose average age was fifteen. The most frightening aspect of the
article was the statement that most of these children were never
reported as missing.

About the same time, a television commercial appeared showing a
father driving his child to a deserted area, abandoning him on the
road, and driving away. The commercial advertised a counseling
center that attempted to help families deal with their problems before
they reached that level.

The exposure of physical and sexual abuse inflicted not only on adolescents but on very young children as well was a horrifying discovery. How could anyone hurt children in these unimaginable ways? How could someone in the family be the perpetrator of such crimes? But even worse was the discovery that our children could not tell us what was happening. They had to endure monstrous damage to their bodies, their emotions, and their very souls without being able to ask for our help. Their fears of retaliation were too great, their terror too overwhelming. They could only attempt to hide within themselves, learning inescapable messages of victimization.

The experience of sexual abuse is like soul murder. We've murdered the souls of far too many of our children. With help, some will heal. But too many will live lifeless lives, haunted by pain and fear, terrified by the past, overwhelmed by the horror of flashbacks and night terrors that recreate the memories of events beyond endurance.

THE COST TO WOMEN

As American society has become steadily more sexually open and permissive, the creative intimacy of sexuality has all too often become a nightmare of aggressive, violent behavior. This is most vividlly described in the experience of date rape, a new phenomenon of the 1980s. The date rapist says, "I've a right to a sexual experience because I took you out on a date. Whether you want it or not doesn't matter. I paid, now you pay." Young women have paid and paid dearly for these changes in our sexual morality.

Domestic violence has threatened the safety and welfare of far too many women. The growing number of shelters available to victims of violence in the home are painful reminders of the horror of physical abuse in the family.

In the 1980s more than 50 percent of women are engaged in the work force, holding down part-time or full-time jobs. But most of these women are also continuing to care for the family and managing lives full of conflicting demands and overburdened with responsibilities. Significant numbers are suffering from major stresses on the job, including sexual harrassment and discrimination. Women continue to be underpaid and undervalued in the workplace. The emotional depression that many women suffer may be directly related to the experience of being a woman in present-day American culture.

THE GROWING PROBLEMS OF POVERTY

As the gap between rich and poor deepened and widened in the 1980s, more and more women and children fell into the poverty population. We have produced a new generation of children growing up without adequate food, shelter, education, or emotional support. They will have very few choices for living. Their scars will be indelible.

The poverty population is most poignantly and visibly evident in the growing numbers of the homeless. We see them in shelters run by the government or private charities; we see them standing around or sitting or lying in the streets and parks and other public places; we see helplessness and hopelessness in every aspect of their lives. They are entirely removed from any vestige of family living.

AIDS

As the 1980s drew to a close, we faced the most difficult legacy of our drug abuse and sexual permissiveness, a legacy that affected not only men but women and children as well—acquired immune deficiency syndrome (AIDS). We knew that we were seeing only the beginning of the AIDS epidemic, which has become painfully manifest in the 1990s. None of us will escape the emotional, physical, and financial cost of this dread disease.

The 1980s have brought us to the edge of chaos. If we've finally hit bottom, in Alcoholics Anonymous terms, we've learned that we have to change the way we're living our lives. If we haven't made that decision, we're dangerously close to being destroyed by the continuation of behaviors that are destructive and out of control. The 1990s is the time we must make the choice between living or dying. The future is now.

6

Looking Back and
Looking Ahead

In sixty short years we've moved from the traditional family through
the nuclear family, the fractured family, the child-dominated family
and the single-parent family, the couple family and the blended
family, to perhaps the perpetual family. As we look at this picture of
continuing change, it would be easy to see ourselves as victims of a
society that is rapidly deteriorating. Or we could stand back as
historians and try to understand what's happened to us in these sixty
years. History *can* teach us. In fact, we find clarity and insight only
when we are able to step back from the intensity and confusion of
the immediate situation and examine a broader point of view.
Unexamined history traps us; ignorance causes us to repeat our
mistakes rather than understand them and rectify them.

LOOKING BACK

When one examines the years between 1930 and 1990 in terms of
family patterns, a persistent theme emerges: the critical loss of
parenting and the breakdown of the functioning family.

In the 1930s and 1940s we saw the beginning of the loss of the
father, jobless or away at war, as the principal authority figure in the
family. At the same time the mother's entrance into the work force

meant another loss to the family. Being a parent had begun to change.

In the 1950s we tried to recreate a "societal childhood," an idealized family environment in which parents became their children's friends. Blurred boundaries between parents and children reduced the authority structure in the family. It was the beginning of no parenting.

In the 1960s and 1970s we experienced an explosive and painful "societal adolescence," an inevitable result of the societal childhood of the previous decade. The authority structure collapsed in the home, the church, the school, and the government. Without a visible authority in the home or society to supply limits and boundaries, adolescents could not move into adulthood. The task of the adolescent is to separate from us. Our task is to remain steadfast and firm in our requirements for adulthood. They need us to "stay put" while they move on. They must have our responsible attention to guide them toward maturation and our modeling of adulthood as worth the struggle and the pain to achieve. But many of us, confused by changes in society, had given up being models of adulthood and guides on the path, so our young people remained fixated in their struggle, as did our society.

In the 1980s we tried to move out of our societal adolescence into a responsible "societal adulthood." Unfortunately our societal adolescence was too well supported by narcissism and drug and alcohol abuse to make that transition easy. Narcissism kept us from relating to and being responsible for others, and it denied the reality of the hard work needed for growth. Drug and alcohol abuse encouraged us to be entirely self-absorbed and out of control, oblivious to the rules and regulations of society. Credit and credit cards allowed us to play now, pay later. The road to responsible adulthood was blocked.

LOOKING AT THE 1990s

In the 1990s we will continue to struggle toward a societal adulthood, in which our adolescent preoccupations will be set aside in favor of an adulthood that is responsible for others as well as ourselves. The struggle will continue to be difficult because we are an addicted society. We're addicted not only to drugs and alcohol but also to food, television, achievement, work, health, gambling, shopping, money, and power. We're still looking for something—anything that will bring us happiness. We've been searching for a long time, but each road has come to a dead end, and we are weary.

Like all addicts who reach an ultimate bottom in their descent toward oblivion, we're beginning to feel our helplessness, which means we may be finally on the first rung of the climb to recovery.

Recovery requires two things of us: (1) we must recognize our need to change and (2) we must realize we cannot change in personal isolation. Our addictive, narcissistic, adolescent self must give way to a responsible, caring, adult self, and we must become reconnected to the community of others. There are no other choices to make. Within our family structures, we must have people willing to be responsible parents. These are the only conditions in which societal adulthood can be achieved.

As we've seen, in the last sixty years, the family has gone through painful disruptions and major breakdowns, making it difficult to perform its necessary function of caring for the young. The responsibility of being a parent has become more complex, while the loss of the extended family and the weakening of community structures have greatly reduced parental support. A barrage of information about parenting, whether through books or unrealistic family television shows, has been confusing rather than enlightening. Economic pressures have forced both parents into dual roles of parent and provider, reducing the time and energy available for parenting to dangerously low levels. Single parents have even less time and strength for being with their children.

If there's been a purpose to all the changes we have endured, it has been to remind us of the necessity and the miracle of the family. Our responsibility to our children is our highest responsibility. They cannot grow into responsible adults without our guidance and care, and society cannot survive without future responsible generations.

Early in this century, we took on the task of protecting our children from industrial rape. In passing child labor laws we defended their right to be children, not slaves of a mechanized society. Once again, we are confronted with another danger threatening our children. They need our love and protection from a society that doesn't seem to value them enough to provide for their well-being.

We've learned enough in these last sixty years to provide what children need to grow into responsible adults. The basic question is whether we'll take seriously the incredible struggle we've experienced and act upon what we've learned. The choice must be made by each of us on behalf of our whole society.

THE ROAD WE'VE COME

1920s: Before the Depression
Traditional Family
- father as head of household
- mother as caretaker of home
- presence of extended family

1930s: Great Depression
- father losing authority and prestige
- mother moving toward paid labor and more authority
- children suffering insecurity and helplessness leading to fear and passivity

1940s: World War II and Korean War
- father absent at war or factory
- mother more absent in work force
- shortage of gasoline and consumer goods
- importance of family and neighborhood

1950s: Peace and Prosperity
Nuclear Family
- geographic mobility and loss of extended family
- togetherness
- permissiveness, parents as friends of children, beginning of no parenting
- availability of consumer goods and lure of television

1960s: Vietnam War
Fractured Family
- civil rights movement
- women's liberation
- sexual revolution
- human-potential movement
- adolescents rebelling against authority
- parents losing credibility and control
- arrival of drugs

1970s: Watergate Scandal and Inflation
Child-Dominated Family
Single-Parent Family
- children controlling the family
- increasing divorce rate and mothers leaving home
- decline of church and school
- increasing use of drugs
- narcissism

1980s: Increasing Violence in Society
Couple Family
Blended Family
Perpetual Family
- destructiveness of drugs
- preadolescent violence
- adolescent suicide
- runaway and abused children
- women suffering violence and the double pressures of work and home
- increasing poverty and AIDS

PART 2

WHAT WE HAVE LEARNED

7

About Young Children

In these sixty years of change, a psychological awakening has radically changed our ideas about the emotional growth of human beings, especially the growth of young children. Prior to the 1930s we tended to view children as needing to be taken care of physically, that is, having their food, shelter, and clothing provided. We also tried to educate them, protect them from danger, and train them to become responsible adults. In that basic training process, we saw our parental role as that of teacher and authority figure as well as guardian of our children.

We did not concern ourselves much with our children's emotional life. In fact, had the subject been brought to our attention, we'd have denied that children had much emotional life at all. In our children-are-to-be-seen-and-not-heard philosophy, we saw children as needing "shaping" for adulthood, rather than understanding of their growth process. We didn't recognize the multitude of intense feelings that children experience from birth on, and we didn't hear their cries for a responsive interchange with us. They were, after all, so very little. What feelings could they have, other than simply needing to be taken care of?

Sometimes, however, we viewed children as miniature adults who just needed the chance to become bigger. In other words, they already knew what they were supposed to do. If they didn't behave properly, it was because they were defiant and irresponsible. For such behaviors, they needed to be punished.

Essentially, then, we had two views of children: (1) that they were emotionless and needed to be taught how to become responsible adults and (2) that they were already miniature adults who occasionally needed to be punished into submission.

FREUD'S VIEW OF CHILDREN

We were shocked out of that worldview by the teachings of Sigmund Freud. Freud brought us a new picture of the emotional life of children and the experience of growing into adulthood. He brought a new vocabulary into our lives: ego, id, super ego, instincts, the unconscious, oedipal conflict, penis envy, castration complex, latency, ego ideal, and the ego defenses including repression, projection, reaction formation, fixation, regression, disavowal, denial, and intellectualization. His most popularized contribution was the Freudian "slip." All these concepts became part of the language we used to explain ourselves and our children.

We became conscious of our unconscious; we began to "listen" to our dreams; we decided we'd been wrong in the way we were training our children. We became enlightened in psychological ways and educated in psychological concepts. In many ways psychology became the new theology of the twentieth century. It offered a description of human nature and an explanation of our very being. Psychology showed us a new way to behave and predicted a "fulfilled life" if we would follow its path. We were fascinated and ready to make significant changes in our lives.

Freud's gift to us was his understanding of the emotional lives of children. He introduced us to a developmental model of growth that has been the prelude to other significant contributions to our knowledge of the experience of growing up. We understand today that the marvelously formed body we possess is matched by a highly complex psychological self, which is matched by an astonishingly available spiritual self.

We've learned that a child is to be loved, nurtured, guided, protected, and taught how to grow through an exceedingly difficult maze of experiences into responsible adulthood. Neither emotionless objects nor miniature adults, children are cherished beings who must have our care and attention if they are to utilize the gift of life.

PERMISSIVENESS

We took the knowledge we'd discovered, however, and ran too far with it. The destination we reached was more shaped by popular psychology than acquired through careful data gathering and longitudinal study. In the 1950s Freud had convinced us of the importance of the first few years of life in the forming of a human being. We determined that our young children would have the best possible early life experiences. They would feel loved, valued, and important, and thereby we would ensure their healthy psychological growth into adulthood.

To that end we became advocates of permissiveness. Permissiveness meant we were determined not to interfere with our children's "healthy" growth. "Not interfering" meant not restricting, inhibiting, or denying our children what they wanted. If their ego was to be strong, we would ensure that strength by making them feel special. If their self-image was to be confident and assured, we would supply new stimuli to provide experiences that were confidence building. We would reduce rules and regulations to prevent their growth from being hampered by artificial conventions. Instead of being parents to our children, we would become their friends.

Our permissiveness had some positive aspects. It was time we realized that children need our understanding of their emotional life. It was essential we recognize childhood as a developmental period of growth, a time of lessons and experiences to be lived and understood. It was crucial that we learn how important a loving, nurturing environment is to the well-being of children.

But in our eagerness to provide the kind of psychological environment we thought our children needed, we lost sight of some of the equally essential ingredients of parenting. We'd come to understand that children were not emotionless objects, and we decided that we would "permit" them to become fully emotional beings. But in our obsession with providing the freedom of self-expression, we became less able to provide limits and structure. In our desire to remove restrictions, we lost sight of a child's need for boundaries. In permitting the feeling of one's emotions, we neglected to teach society's limits on the expression of such emotions and the ability to choose between feelings felt and feelings expressed.

We wanted to create a world of unconditional love and safety. Instead we found ourselves living in a chaotic world in which the children were increasingly in charge, with no one able to discern what needed to be done for anyone. We didn't realize how frightening it might be to our children to grow up without the loving safety and control of wise parents. We didn't realize that with all our permissiveness and efforts to provide a free, enriched environment, such an environment did not *permit* our children to grow.

Our permissiveness was originally focused on our younger population, the child from birth to four years of age. In time permissiveness spread to all ages, making us truly victims of an anything-goes, do-you-own-thing society, which was the ultimate destination of our permissive path. In our zeal to produce the best of all possible worlds, we had created a fictionalized universe that had no correspondence in the world outside the home. Our children could not make the transition from home to the "real" world outside because they had no tools for living in a community with others. Our support of their "specialness" had made it impossible for them to live in an environment in which they were not seen as unique. Gradually we learned that our permissiveness was wrong.

THE IMPACT OF DAY CARE

At the same time that we were advocating permissiveness, we were placing our young children in day care, which seemed to support our second premise about children, that they are miniature adults who don't have to have two parents around to love and help them into adulthood. Instead we turned them over to all-too-often exhausted, underpaid day-care workers, who attempted to look after too many children. The children struggled to survive in a world that did not meet their needs. Children are not miniature adults. They cannot secure an adequate place in society without the help of parents who understand that they need parental care and commitment.

At the present time, day care, no matter how good it is, cannot provide what two active, caring parents can. The ratio of child to helper is simply too great. Our understanding of what children need to grow into mature adulthood mandates that we find ways to support good parental care (for example, paid maternity leaves for both mothers and fathers or financial support for single mothers to be at home with their newborns for an extended time). Where good parental care is not available, the needs of young children must become a priority in building some kind of support system for their growth. The price of not providing adequate, early care for children is one that all of society will pay when uncared-for children reach adulthood.

SELF-CONTROL AND CHOICE

A research project conducted by Walter Mischel at Columbia University offers us a vivid picture of what young children need in their journey toward adulthood. Mischel was concerned with the capacity of preschool children to delay gratification as a predictor of adolescent competence. As reported in *Science* magazine, 26 May, 1989, Mischel and his colleagues designed an experiment in which four-year-old subjects were offered two treats, one obviously more attractive than the other. They were told they could have the smaller, less attractive treat, a couple of small cookies, at any time. But if they could wait fifteen minutes until the experimenter returned to the room, they could have the more attractive treat, five pretzels.

The key to successful waiting was distraction. The more successful children understood they would be less frustrated waiting if they could distract themselves. They did so in a variety of ways: they talked to themselves; they sang songs; they shut their eyes; they picked their noses; they fell asleep—all in the service of delaying their gratification.

In a ten-year follow-up of this study, when these same four-year-olds were fourteen, researchers found that the children who delayed longer when rewards were visible were considered by their parents to be significantly more attentive, more able to concentrate, more goal oriented, and more intelligent. Their parents also thought they were better able to handle temptation, frustration, and stress. The researcher's conclusions were simple. If you are able to exert self-control, you have a choice. If you cannot exert self-control, your choices become very limited.

The linkage of self-control with wider choice is an essential lesson for American society. We've been prescribing no self-control by

maintaining a permissive, anything-goes, do-you-own-thing philosophy. No wonder we feel so choiceless and so powerless!

Research projects such as Mischel's show us what we must do to
help our young children grow into adulthood. The lesson of self-
control is most appropriately and effectively learned in early childhood. *The way to teach self-control, however, is to model self-control.*
We cannot expect our children to learn any kind of self-control if we
as parents are not demonstrating the value and reward for such
behavior in our own lives. When we believe we can unleash any and
all of our own feelings, we're sending an unforgettable message to
our children to do the same thing. When we believe we can subtly or
openly defy the laws and regulations of our society, we must reckon
with the fact that our children will imitate our lawless behavior.

If we delay the teaching of self-control to young children and try
to introduce it later, we'll have to use far more punitive measures
with far less effectiveness, as we have already painfully discovered.

The societal changes of the last sixty years have clearly demonstrated what happens to family life when self-control is missing.
Lack of self-control inhibits any possibility for the attainment of
successful adulthood. In addition, it guarantees continued instability
within the family until parents learn the connection between the
freedom to grow and the ability to demonstrate self-control. To
permit young children *not* to learn that lesson is to condemn them to
a life without choice, without the ability to live in a world of others,
and without the prerequisite for their successful entry into the next
phase of their development.

8

About Children in Latency

Traditionally, children between five and twelve are considered to be in the latency period of development. Those children today who actually experience latency, however, are a disappearing breed. The latency years used to be seen as a quiet time of growth and development in which nothing much happened. All the sexual curiosity that Freud described in young children was supposed to become dormant during latency. Children were to go to school, help around the house, play with their friends and family, and stay out of trouble.

In the past, the latency period allowed a lovely balance between work and play. It was considered a time of productivity and mastery when children learned those survival skills that would allow them to control and manipulate their environment. Basically, they learned how to be responsible members of the family and the community. Latency was also a time for spontaneous, creative, imaginative play and the development of deep bonds of companionship between parents and children.

When the American economy was more agrarian, children in the latency period were expected to participate fully in the farm work and household chores to help maintain the family. In fact, the family was often dependent on their productivity to survive. Everyone in the family expected to work together, and when the work was finished, everyone gathered for more playful activities.

As society became more industrialized, the tasks of latency-age children began to change. No longer responsible for chores around the farm, children in cities and suburbs concentrated more on survival skills in the home—learning how to cook a meal, wash the dishes, clean the house, wash and mend clothing, take care of the yard, make simple mechanical repairs, handle money, shop for necessities, cooperate with others, and respect community property. Children needed to learn basic lessons about responsible, cooperative living in the family and survival in the world, and latency was the best and most effective time to learn those lessons. It was a very workable arrangement.

But in recent history, especially since World War II, three changes in family life have altered the latency experience for most children. The first change is the reduction of the actual time parents spend teaching life skills and cooperative living to their children because the parents are working outside the home. The second change is the substitution of organized activities and enrichment experiences outside the family to make up for the loss of available time in the family. The third change is the fast forwarding of these five-to-twelve-year-olds into early adolescent experiences.

REDUCTION OF PARENTAL TIME WITH CHILDREN

The prevalence today of dual-income families means that parents and children no longer have much direct experiential contact of working together on the care and maintenance of the family. Now such tasks are performed by nonfamily members (if they are done at all), who usually have significantly less time for, and interest in, the job than parents had. In some cases, where non-English-speaking people are providing child care, language barriers interfere with the transmission of information and the development of cooperative family living. Similarly the opportunity for imaginative, playful, spontaneous experiences within the family has been greatly reduced by the loss of the parents' available time.

In single-parent households, the single parent is usually working at least part-time, resulting in an even more profound loss of opportunity for children to learn from and play with a parent. The loss is experienced by both the single parent and the child involved, each sensing that moments of unstructured companionship are deeply interfered with by the lack of time.

In divorce situations, the problem may be exacerbated by competitive issues between the former spouses. Often the noncustodial parent tries to offer the children pleasurable times and play experiences rather than more "serious" times of chores and responsibility, as a way of dealing with their mutal concerns of separation and loss. But as work and "fun" are polarized, resentments build, and children are caught in a web of parental rivalry. The little time available for parents to be with children is filled with negative, combative emotions instead of the pleasure of being together.

SUBSTITUTION OF ENRICHMENT FOR BASICS

Because time has become such a precious commodity in our family life and because the loss of time is so painful, parents today often sacrifice some of the basic, learning tasks of the latency period for more organized, nonfamily activities such as athletics and enrichment classes as a way of helping children deal with the loss of parental time. Such activities allow parents to feel they are providing their children with growth-producing experiences, while at the same time helping them to become more independent. Though they may not be directly involved in the activity, many parents spend a great deal of time enabling their children to have these extra enrichments. In fact, there's nothing wrong with our desire to provide children with new learning experiences, except when we go to an extreme in our zeal to be helpful.

Little League baseball, which began as a backyard sport, has become an organized institution with schedules that in many households take over family life between May and September. Ice hockey and soccer have followed, so the entire year is filled with athletic possibilities for the five-to-twelve set. These athletic programs provide the opportunity for skill building and team participation. But they also change sports from spontaneous play into competitive play, which is considerably less playful and much more intense. The empty neighborhood lot, formerly the scene of hours of unstructured play, has been replaced by designated areas where organized sports are tightly scheduled, involving local business sponsors and community participation. Creative play is lost in the complexity of organized competition, and spontaneous family play is often replaced by practice sessions. Parents become observers; some parents become critics; children become performers; none of these positions calls for playful interactions.

For children who are not sports minded there are other kinds of organized activities—music lessons, dancing lessons, language lessons, art classes, computer classes, religion classes, and "Great Books" classes. We work hard to provide enrichments for our children. No cost is too great, no effort too much. We are committed to their growth and development.

The problem is one of time. Given the lack of available time that parents have with their children today, if we provide these extra experiences, good in themselves, will we still find time for the critical and essential learning of latency? The answer probably lies in the numbers of children who are not prepared to grow up because they haven't yet learned how to live in the world.

Latency must be a time of learning the basic, fundamental skills of living in the world. It is a period when we develop lifelong attitudes toward work, play, and companionship. It is a natural time for learning because children are curious, interested, excited, and ready for new experiences. The home and school become essential partners in the learning that characterizes the latency period, each having specific tasks to be mastered and each providing opportunities for cooperative, responsible living.

Learning to take responsibility is the cornerstone of the latency experience: responsibility to the self in experiences of learning both at home and in school; responsibility to the family in shared, cooperative, caretaking tasks at home; and responsibility to others and their property in school and in the community.

The latency experience also provides the essential bridge between childhood and adolescence. The knowledge and skills acquired during latency enable children to approach adolescence with confidence and assurance. Without this bridge of experience and knowledge, children move from early childhood into the crisis of adolescence without any preparation or foundation, as if they were trying to cross a chasm on a frayed rope bridge.

The latency period became an endangered time for children when we decided they would enjoy extra, enriching activities far more than learning the basic fundamentals of living. Those fundamentals seemed more like chores, and we did not want to burden our children with them. We tried to spare them the more mundane aspects of living. "They're only young once" was our rationalization for excusing them from participation in responsible family living. But this was clearly *our* view, not theirs.

Children between five and twelve enjoy helping others, and they like learning to be competent. They're eager to participate with us in the tasks of the home; they prefer working actively with us to watching television passively in the same room. They also prefer our companionship to our absence; they like who we are, and they feel important to us when we share our time with them. They like to play with us, and when we take the time for simple shared pleasures, they feel valued and loved. They take pride in their parents and their family and have a strong sense of "our values," "our way of doing things," and "our family."

Within a few short years they will be totally uninterested in helping us do anything. For this time alone, they're our greatest fans and helpers. If we deny them the opportunity to be helpful, if we minimize their need to be responsible, we take away their opportunity to develop competence and confidence, leaving them with a great void where there should be a solid anchoring in experience.

If we do not spend time with them in companionable and playful ways, we deny them opportunities for intimacy with parents who love and enjoy them. Spending time together conveys a simple, straightforward message. It says, "I love you enough to want to spend time with you. You're important to me." Not spending time together also carries an undeniable message: "You're not important enough for me to set aside time for you." Too many children are receiving that message.

Some children have had too many enrichment experiences and too little acquisition of skills, leaving them interesting to talk to but lacking in fundamental knowledge and awareness, as if they had eaten a rich dessert without eating the main course first. Other children have neither the knowledge of basic skills nor the experience of enrichment because of limited contact with parents or parenting persons. Their ability to succeed in this world is greatly hampered by not having someone who is sufficiently available to teach them these basic skills.

For some children, the essential learning of latency is connected to survival on the "street." These are children who are already involved in illegal activities, and for them there is virtually no future

because there's never been a present time in which they've been
properly cared for.

FAST FORWARDING TO ADOLESCENCE

The third change that has altered the latency experience is the
crowding of the latency years with experiences more properly be-
longing to adolescence. Suddenly our ten-to-twelve-year-olds were
talking about dating, drugs, x-rated films, and boy/girl parties. They
were becoming more rebellious and critical. They were beginning to
use alcohol and drugs. It was as if adolescence had invaded latency,
shrinking the time frame and squeezing the latency period into a
tiny package between the important concerns of early childhood and
the frightening experiences of adolescence.

We've called these casualties of insufficient latency experiences,
"hurried children," and hurried they were. They sped through
latency as if they were on a train that was not making any stops.
They entered adolescence without any knowledge of who they were,
what they could do, and whom they could count on. "Overfed" or
"malnourished" in terms of learning experiences by well-intentioned
or indifferent parents, they were allowed to race ahead with no one
to stop them or say no to them in their urgency to follow a faster
track. They were ripe for trouble.

Much as we'd like to deny these facts, the truth is that some of
these children who are so intent on fast forwarding into adolescence
are already abusing alcohol and drugs. Some of our preteen children
are out of control in their behaviors and attitudes. They've become
abusive to other children and adults as well as to their parents. Some
have become destructive of both personal and public property.

Parental permissiveness and failure to insist on the development of
responsible behaviors have given our latency-age children a confused,
mixed message about life. Sometimes we tell them to "just have fun"
and forget all this "heavy stuff" about responsibility. Then we get
angry with them for not behaving properly. They don't know which
message we mean.

We also seem to have forgotten that children learn from adults'
actions. If we ourselves are cooperative, responsible citizens, then
our children will learn what is expected of them. If we don't model
appropriate behaviors, our children won't learn them or use them.

THE IMPORTANCE OF THE LATENCY PERIOD

What we've learned about latency is quite simple: the learning appropriate to latency must happen. We can't allow our children to miss this opportunity to learn how to live in the world. The proper latency experience has not taken place until children learn the skills of survival, cooperation, and responsibility. They must be allowed to discover the value and pleasure of knowledge, work, play, and companionship if they are to grow into well-balanced adults. At no other time are they so ready to integrate and use these life lessons.

The connection of success in latency and success in adulthood is very powerful. The challenge for us is to provide the essential latency learning to children who do not have parents or parenting persons to assist them through this period of time. These are the lost children who will become lost adults if we don't find the means to help them. At the other extreme are those children who are seen as too special to have to engage in such basic behaviors. The neglect of fundamental latency experiences for these children means that they also are deprived of the opportunity to live as cooperative adult members of society. Both of these groups of children are in danger of not being able to develop into well-functioning adults.

During early childhood, children learn crucial lessons of *self-control*. During the latency period, they learn how to *survive and be responsible*. In adolescence, as we shall see, their task is to *separate from us and enter adulthood*. Each stage builds on the next, providing children with a strong foundation to be able to live in a complex and difficult world.

In acknowledging the importance of the latency period, we recognize that attitudes formed then have lifelong consequences. Noncompetitive play, encouraged in the latency period, tends to produce an adult who recognizes the value of play as an ongoing source of pleasure. The sense of competence and mastery that occurs in doing a job well in latency tends to produce an adult who can enjoy work and see it as an expression of personal worth. The experience of cooperative living in latency helps create an adult who will insist on the value of working together at home, on the job, and in community efforts.

The bonds that are created in latency between parents and children who play, work, love, and dream together are unforgettable lessons about the basic and wonderful gifts of life. If we do not provide these experiences for our children during latency, we deny them the foundation they must have to form their own bonds of intimacy in adulthood.

All the developmental phases begin in a kind of review period, in which previously learned lessons are reinforced and the person is solidly positioned for the next phase of growth. For the latency-age child who's already learned some lessons of self-control in the first years of life, the years between five and seven are opportunities for the reinforcement of self-control, which is now practiced outside the family as well. With that lesson firmly in place, a child can focus full energy on all the other learnings of latency (competence, responsibility, work, play, companionship) in the years between eight and twelve, as preparation for adolescence. In fact, we will work on these latency issues for the rest of our lives.

The tasks of latency are so profoundly important for successful living that we must not shortchange this experience for our children. In latency we preview the adult who is to come. The more skills for living we are able to impart at this stage in development, the more we can ensure the success of that future adult. Conversely, failure to impart these skills creates an adult who is always struggling just to survive.

As the latency years come to a close, the first signs of adolescence predict the last lesson of childhood. Separation issues begin to show themselves in the waning years of latency. Our children experience a growing sense of independence and autonomy that signals the overture of adolescence. We watch them starting to cross the bridge into adolescence, and we know that the final struggle in the process of becoming an adult has begun.

9

About Adolescents

Adolescents have gained a bad reputation. Parents used to consider them troublesome and annoying, a mild cross to bear until they reached adulthood. We saw their behavior as an expected flexing of teenage muscles that was irritating but seldom destructive. We could live with the situation because we knew it was temporary.

But over the past thirty years we've wrung our hands and felt like captives of a new "enemy" called the adolescent. In the 1960s we were introduced to this new creature, who was defiant, rebellious, and seemingly determined to undermine all our rules and regulations. We entered a new age of chaotic change heralded by long hair, loud music, drug abuse, open hostility, and destructive behaviors.

Not every adolescent became the "enemy." But there were sufficient numbers of them to challenge the essence of our societal and family values. We didn't know how to handle the rebelliousness; we didn't know the danger of drug and alcohol abuse; we were stunned by behavior and language that would have been forbidden to us in our adolescence.

What was happening? Why was it happening? What did we do wrong?—these were the questions we constantly raised. In our confusion and frightened helplessness, we started to comply with adolescent demands for fewer rules and more freedom and tried to convince ourselves that "they" (the adolescents) were probably right. After all, it was a new generation and things were changing—right? We didn't understand that it was an old problem in a new setting, so we chose to accommodate adolescents' demands. But still the problem persisted. Our accommodation turned to anger and eventually became rage. We were at war with our adolescents.

Throughout the 1970s and 1980s we turned to psychology to help us with the problems of adolescence, as we had with earlier stages of human life. We learned all about the experience of adolescence; we formed parent groups to talk about our adolescent children. But we were still uncertain about our role as parents to these children. We weren't sure how to discipline them, and we seemed to have lost our way in knowing how to relate to them. Parents began to dread the years when their children would become adolescent. When adolescent experiences began to invade latency, and our younger children started to show signs of defiance, parents felt utterly overwhelmed!

SEPARATION

If we can take a more realistic, objective look at adolescence, we see that it is basically the same experience it always has been. The most important concern of adolescence is separation, and most adolescent behavior is subsumed under that heading. Adolescents face two fundamental, overlapping phases of separation: (1) separating from their childhood in early adolescence and (2) separating from their parents and family in later adolescence. All the defiant, rebellious, crazy, unpredictable behavior parents see in adolescents is in the service of these two phases of separation.

Separation from Childhood

Early adolescence is the time to leave childhood and regroup one's forces in order to face the larger, later challenge of separation from parents and entry into adulthood. As adolescents separate from their childhood, both their conscious struggle for maturity and their unconscious desire to remain a child become apparent. It is not easy to grow up, and the changes required of adolescents are difficult and confusing.

Physiological changes herald adolescence. Bodies change, voices change, sexual concerns emerge. The potency of sexuality is the propellant toward adulthood. The sexual curiosity of the young child becomes the powerful sexual drive of the adolescent. Suddenly our children are facing feelings that are overwhelming and confusing to them. At the same time they sense that such feelings are private and inappropriate to share with us. The matter of sexuality represents a giant leap from childhood into an abyss of strong emotions.

In adolescence, our children enter the impossible world of trying to control the uncontrollable! They have no control over their own particular biological clock. The physiological changes of adolescence occur on an inner, genetic schedule, not on demand. As sexual feelings become more powerful, one's whole body can feel overwhelmed and unfamiliar. Strong hormonal changes produce strong emotional responses. No wonder adolescents show such nonproductive and aberrant behavior! It's not surprising they need to spend endless amounts of time alone or with their friends, who are going through similar changes. They're trying to gain any degree of control they can.

If adolescents are lucky, they enter puberty around twelve or thirteen and feel like one of the crowd. If they enter very early, at nine or ten, or very late, at sixteen or seventeen, they feel isolated and uncomfortable. Locker rooms can be places of dread for the adolescent who matures too early or too late.

The unconscious desire of adolescents to remain children is an understandable response to such profound physiological and emotional changes. It's a normal and natural resistance to a process that takes over, moving adolescents toward adulthood as inexorably as a wave moves toward the shore. Sometimes the process feels very stormy indeed, and adolescents use any device they can to avoid it or slow it down. They act silly or they create terrible messes in their rooms. What could be more convincing to parents that they are still children? They avoid us or speak to us in monosyllables so that we'll surely not know what is happening to them. They withdraw from affectionate responses to us, because distance allows them to hide the changes in their bodies.

During adolescence, parents see minute-by-minute changes in their offspring. One moment, he or she is a child who can't be expected to be responsible for much of anything. The next moment he or she reveals a glimpse of the responsible and helpful adult who is growing within. There seems to be no middle ground and no way to predict which one will be around at any particular time.

A scheme that vividly describes this splitting between the child that was and the adult that is to come is as follows:

> Twelve is a lot like two,
> Thirteen is a lot like three,
> Fourteen is a lot like four,
> Fifteen is a lot like five,
> Sixteen is a lot like six.

It's as if the concerns of childhood return during adolescence to be addressed once more. Matters of trust, autonomy, sexuality, and identity are integral parts of the adolescent experience and are repeatedly faced and challenged. "You don't trust me" is the basic battle cry of the adolescent. "Don't you think I can take care of myself?" is a new demand for autonomy. "Leave me alone" attests to all of the changes and sums up the pain and the challenge of adolescence.

We cannot "do" our children's adolescence for them. In effect, we have both to leave them alone *and* be there with them in the process. On the one hand we have to recognize the child who doesn't want to grow up, who feels frightened and unready. That child needs our support and encouragement, as if we were a good cheering section in a hard-fought game, for no one feels more ambivalent and ashamed about their "childishness" than adolescents. On the other hand, we have to recognize that they despise their neediness and dependence. Their behavior may be immature, but they cannot bear to have us see them as children. They require us to provide a safe place, with limits and structure, so they can make this essential transition out of childhood. Without the structure, they're adrift in a heavy sea of far too many emotional and physiological changes.

Their message to us in this first of their two separation phases is, "Help me but don't save me! Help me to leave the safety of my childhood and enter this unknown road to adulthood. But don't save me from the struggle, the uncertainty, and the confusion. Let me know, by your support and encouragement, that I can make it. Be there, within reach but not too close. Supply the net that will keep me from falling into dangerous territory, until I'm ready to leave and be on my own."

This first separation experience, separation from childhood, occurs during the early years of adolescence and is repeated many times until the next plateau is reached. Because it comes on the heels of all the competency concerns that children worked through during the latency period, it often seems discouraging to parents to see young adolescents appear to be struggling so much.

Whatever happened to my capable ten-year-old? a parent will ask. Where is the child who always loved to help me? How did the child who used to like to play and be sociable suddenly become an antisocial recluse?

Separation from Parents

The second phase of separation is painful for both children and parents because it carries so many feelings of loss. The child we love, who has taken up so much of our time and energy, starts to push us away as if we were insignificant, obsolete, and useless. Our wisdom and helpfulness are rejected as the child discovers "truth" from other sources. We look in confusion and anger at the "stranger" who used to think we were the most important people in the world. We may have understood some of the problems in separation from childhood, but this is a different situation. This time *we* are the object of separation; this is separation from *us*.

We wonder what it all means. Will we ever again have the relationship with our children that we used to have? Has all this time and effort been spent simply to say good bye and good luck? It doesn't feel good, and even if we understand intellectually that this separation process has to take place, at a deeper level we may feel abandoned and alone. Unfortunately for most parents, our adolescents begin to leave us in our forties, when we are subject to our own questions about life and what it means. We may be in the middle of our own mid-life crises. It's very bad timing!

The solution looks easy: We should try not to take all of this so personally. Our children are not leaving us, they're leaving what we represent. They don't really think we're inept; it's just that their friends have become essential as a bridge away from home. It's not that our home has suddenly become a halfway house for strangers. It's an inevitable one-foot-in-the-door-one-foot-out-the-door experience for everyone.

Even the most sophisticated parent usually feels the confusion and intensity of this separation. Part of the confusion is the result of a simple strategy that works wonderfully well for our children and miserably for us. The way for our children to separate most effectively from us is to become *as different from us as possible*. They work this strategy to the hilt.

For example, if you work hard, they'll show you how inactive they can be. If you value achievement, they'll manage to get by with C's and D's. If you believe in good grooming, they'll be slobs. If you're efficient, you'll have at least one passive-aggressive child. If you love quiet, they'll behave like bulls in a china shop around the house. If you like classical music, they'll drown you out with hard rock. It's all in the service of separation.

A subtler form of separation occurs when children withdraw from us because they cannot tolerate the comparisons *they* make with us. "My dad is so successful . . . I'll never make it like he has," or "My mom is so attractive and smart . . . I feel like a mess." Much of the withdrawal behavior seen in older children is because of comparisons *they* make in which they come out the loser.

Another way adolescents express their separation from parents is through their use of language, especially when we make a request for their help. For example: a parent asks her child, "Will you please take out the garbage?" An active child will probably give an answer like, "Why do you always have to ask me to do something when I'm in the midst of . . .?" This is one way of saying no to a request. A more passive child will probably say, "Sure" or grunt, but no action will take place. This is another way of saying no.

But the no is not written in stone. It's really a statement that says, "I'm different from you. I need to establish my independence; I need to separate and this is one way I have to show you I'm different. But don't take it at face value. I'm not being disobedient. I'm just trying desperately to hang on to the difference between us. I'm new at this separating game, and I don't know how to play it very well. I really will take out the garbage, but first I have to say no!"

Older adolescents also try to make separation easier for us by unconsciously becoming obnoxious. That way, they figure, we'll be delighted to see them grow up and leave home. Second-semester seniors in high school are notoriously difficult to deal with. But then, their separation is imminent!

The separation process begins in early childhood, becomes highly intensified during adolescence, and continues throughout life. It must occur if children are to grow up. It's never easy; it usually involves strong feelings of sadness, anger, and abandonment. Much of the separation process during adolescence is unconscious on the children's part. Therefore it doesn't help to let them know we understand they're trying to separate because it would only make them feel exposed and uncomfortable.

What *does* help is for us to recognize what it's like for our children to leave us, that they find it hard to separate and frightening to move into the adult world. For them it's truly like a second birth. The umbilical cord is cut; the support system of the womb is gone; the moment to breathe and live is *now*. The total dependence of the baby, voiced in that first human cry, is echoed in the silent cry of the adolescent leaving home. Adolescents fight that vulnerability with all their strength. In their struggle to live they must push aside any reminders of their neediness in order to take that final leap toward independence. We represent all the dependence they must leave behind, so we become easy targets for all the fear and desperation of this final breaking away. They cover their grief and fear with various forms of bravado, hostility, and indifference. They'd rather die than let anyone know how sad and ineffective they feel. They require that we know and understand without ever letting them know we know.

Adolescence has been a recognized process for generations. As a result of the changes in the last sixty years, we became afraid of it and unsure of ourselves as parents. We didn't know what to do in the face of all the challenges to our authority. Consequently we couldn't provide the limits and structure our children needed. In our confusion, we lost sight of the fact that children have always confronted and challenged their parents in this last stage of childhood. Children need to let go of the safety and support of the family; parents need both to be present for the child and to release the child they've supported and cared for. The means for accomplishing this goal differ for each side.

Children need to push us away, making us the "bad guy" who's hanging on to them, whether we are or not. They'll portray us in any negative light they can as a means to separate. They need to set *us* up as the "enemy" in order to justify their leaving.

Our job is be there until the hard work of parenting is accomplished. Then we can let go. What irony! We work endless hours for a goal that vanishes at the moment of achievement. We have to provide a kind of exquisite control for our adolescents in which we structure and limit them at the same time we stand back and release them, and we must do all of this while remaining unaffected by accusations of not letting go. Ours is a very hard task.

THE PROBLEMS OF ADOLESCENTS

The problems we're currently facing with the adolescent population are these:

1. deficits incurred in earlier developmental periods, particularly the loss of essential experiences of parental care
2. separation and divorce of parents at the time when adolescents need to be the ones who are separating
3. drug and alcohol abuse
4. uncertainties about the future in terms of identity questions
5. the indefinite prolongation of adolescence into adulthood

Deficits from early developmental periods cause problems for the adolescent who needs to separate. These earlier periods are like building blocks that support the separation process. Without them as an undergirding, separation becomes more confusing and chaotic. A loss of parental attention creates a deficit in the emotional core of the child. Many children today are not ready to go through the crisis of separation because they've not had enough parental attention in the first place. Without a solid base of self-control and learned survival skills and responsibility, adolescents may separate from their parents, but they'll have difficulty living as capable adults.

When adolescents experience their parents' divorce, their own separation process is upstaged and complicated, and they respond with confusion and anger. Parents are abandoning them just when they need to be the ones to be leaving. Some respond by racing through adolescence as fast as possible, reaching adulthood prematurely without completing the tasks of adolescence. Others dig in their heels and settle in for a prolonged adolescence, refusing to move on to adulthood. Adolescents often feel a responsibility for the parent who is being "left" as well as for younger siblings caught in a divorce. They may sacrifice their own growth for the sake of holding the family together. This delays their own separation and often leads to an accrued intensity of frustration and anger.

Additional problems emerge when separated parents are dating others. If adolescents have difficulty with their own intense sexual feelings, they certainly have no way to deal with those of their parents. Today they are exposed not only to the possibility of parental sexuality; they are experiencing the reality of it through the presence of live-in partners. This creates a situation in which adolescents perceive their parents as peers, not parents. Once again they experience the loss of reliable parental figures to guide them through their adolescent experience.

Drug and alcohol abuse always interferes with growth. Adolescents are much more vulnerable to becoming addicted than adults are. It takes less time for the addiction to take hold, and the experience is far more destructive because it stops their growth and places them in dangerous situations beyond their understanding and control. Adolescents who become involved with drugs and/or alcohol will literally lose the years during which they are addicted. Those years are irretrievable. All the problems of separation will be seen through the murky haze of addicted behavior. None of them will be addressed properly, and they will remain painful and unfinished.

Identity concerns for adolescents pertain chiefly to the question "What am I going to do when I grow up?" In earlier times, this question was more easily answered because children had fewer options to choose from, and they didn't delay their decisions. Today's adolescents are confused by too many choices, and they are fearful lest they make the wrong decision. They are intimidated by competition and worried about how they're going to survive financially. If they complete college, they find that graduation no longer guarantees future employment. (Some attempt to avoid the whole issue by going on to graduate school.) The identity question is very caught up in the current economic situation in this country, over which most people have very little control. It is probable that many individuals will have more than one career as they move through their working years, making the question of identity a lifelong problem rather than an adolescent concern.

The uncertainty of one's identity is also reflected in the prolongation of adolescence into young adulthood. Adolescence used to end at age eighteen. We've now extended it to thirty-three—the latest estimate for the end of adolescence! What used to be a transitional time of six or seven years has been extended to twenty years. The very nature of adolescence and young adulthood is being changed by this extension of time.

In some instances, "children" in their twenties are still attempting to get parental attention either by not leaving home or by returning home after having left. Children return home after graduation from college and stay. Children having difficulties with their marriages move back in with the "folks." Financial problems are usually named as the reason to return home. But some of these adult "children" may be unconsciously saying, "We're not ready to face adult life. The world feels too confusing and we don't know who we are and where we belong."

The prolonging of adolescence also reflects the belief that one should put off growing up as long as possible. The narcissism in the 1970s and 1980s tried to make us feel better by convincing us that adulthood and responsibility for others are unnecessary interferences with one's own pleasure. It's this insistence on one's right to have everything for oneself, without regard for others, that finally makes it impossible for adolescents to move into adulthood. If we as parents continue to follow this narcissistic path, we may eventually create a lifelong adolescence for all and a world in which there are no adults. Life in that kind of world is not worth living.

Adolescents caught by the siren song of narcissism have been given an empty, meaningless picture of life. We do them a terrible injustice by not showing them what adult life really could hold for them in terms of satisfactions and fulfillment. The solution for this problem may be found in the perception of adulthood that we provide for our adolescent children. If they see us in various states of depression, anxiety, fear, and hopelessness, they receive a powerful message that adult life is hardly worth living. Why bother to go through all the struggle to grow up if the end result is hopelessness and meaninglessness. This is fertile ground for the continuation of narcissism as the only solution to feeling better. But if we model adulthood as a time of growth and satisfaction, if we demonstrate our pleasure in caring for others and the world in which we live, if we believe in possibility as well as responsibility, we offer a picture of adulthood that has freedom, meaning, and hope.

It is we adults who must believe enough in the miracle and mystery of life that we can offer adolescents a reason to take the hazardous leap of separation into adulthood. That really means that we must have been willing to have done the same thing ourselves.

10

About Young Adults

Most of the developmental aspects of childhood have remained constant over the years. We know the tasks children must complete if they are to become capable adults. But entry into adulthood and the way we perceive adulthood have changed.

We used to consider people adult at eighteen. The distinctions between the experiences of adolescence and those of adulthood were quite clear. Adolescence was the final growth time for young people, who were still essentially children. It was like having a last fling before taking on the seriousness of the grown-up world and full adult responsibilities. The boundaries were clearly marked, and the consequences of transgressions were understood. Both parents and offspring knew which behaviors were appropriate for adolescence and which for adulthood.

Today we have greatly prolonged adolescence and, as noted earlier, consider that the transition into adulthood can take place anywhere from the age of eighteen to thirty-three. In other words, we haven't quite decided where adolescence ends and adulthood begins. We call this transition period the first stage of adulthood, or young adulthood.

ENTRY INTO ADULTHOOD

Today's adolescents begin engaging in adult behaviors long before they reach chronological adult status. Many have become sexually active; they sometimes live together. They experiment with drugs and alcohol. They seek life experiences not as children but as adults. Their whole demeanor demands adult status. As adolescent experiences had crowded latency, now adult experiences have invaded adolescence. Our permissive society has encouraged adolescents to experiment with adult behaviors before they have the understanding or experience to handle so much freedom. It's something like being in a carnival house of mirrors. Who you are and how you get out is distorted and terrifying. The result of this disruption of an essential growth period has made the transition from adolescence into adulthood confusing at best and catastrophic at worst.

Having been allowed to engage in adult behaviors while they were still children, many adolescents, not surprisingly, face adult responsibilities with the fear and confusion of children. Their sense of identity is confused and unformed. How can they judge their competence in a world they've entered before they were ready? Their confidence in their ability to survive is paper-thin. The adult world seems too much, too soon. They ask, What will I do with my life? Can I support myself? How can I get married and raise a family? Even choosing a college major can be a traumatic experience.

Their struggle is painful to experience and watch. They soothe their fears by recalling former successes, cultivating an air of bravado, and distracting themselves with the "good life." Many begin a lifelong struggle with buying on credit, especially if they've not been taught how to handle money. In their attempts to survive economically as well as emotionally, they buy on time, unable to see beyond today's needs, hoping somehow to stay ahead of disaster. They are easily victimized by the credit system, which encourages them to buy what they want when they want it without having cash in hand. Before they know it, they're in debt beyond their ability to pay. Some don't have any idea how it happened or what went wrong.

Many of these late adolescents in transition into adulthood also abuse alcohol and drugs as a way to avoid adult responsibilities. This age group is particularly vulnerable to such abuse, which may be a continuation of habits begun earlier. The streets and the workplace offer unlimited opportunities for the purchase of drugs. But emotional and physical dependence on alcohol and drugs always prevents growth. No one can become a responsible adult while also being an addict. Addiction demands full attention with little time or energy for anything else. A person can become chronologically adult but remain a child in terms of judgment and conscience, seeking only to avoid getting caught or being made to give up the habit.

Marijuana is a particularly enervating drug, whose abusers are rendered incapable of living productively. A considerable number of adolescents become addicted to marijuana without realizing the cost to their development. Their growth literally stops while they focus on the necessity of supplying their addiction. Their transition to adulthood is unachievable. Cocaine addicts are even narrower in their focus. The high cost of cocaine usually forces addicts to engage in various kinds of illegal activities to pay for their addiction, placing them in extremely dangerous situations beyond their control or capacity to manage. Moreover, cocaine and its cheaper form, crack, are so destructive that some users' lives are finished the moment they become addicted.

Unlike any other transitional time, the entry into adulthood has become a torturous experience for those struggling to achieve it. To become adult requires them to enter fully the world of responsibility, no longer depending on parents for care. The test of adulthood lies in the ability to shift from the narcissistic focus of adolescence to an adult position of care and responsibility for self and others. But everything we present to adolescents attempting to reach adulthood seems to work against their successful entry. Our economy flaunts narcissistic needs as a fundamental "right." Popular psychology glorifies the self without concern for others. Even the church has become involved in issues of psychology and self-growth. Spirituality, faith in God, and concern for our "neighbor" often take a second place to the more absorbing fascination in one's own life and destiny. We've made the entrance into adulthood less desirable than the continuation of adolescence.

If we, as adults, continue to validate the kind of picture of the world that aggrandizes the self without concern for others, we'll make it impossible for these "almost adults" to reach full growth. They still carry with them the narcissism of adolescence. If we don't show them another way to be, they won't be able to let go of the self-absorption that carried them through their teens.

As in all developmental stages, lessons not learned in adolescence will be repeated at a later date. Repetitions will make them easier, but the siren song of permissive narcissism will continue until we as a society find a substitute for this endless preoccupation with the self. The cost to our children in personal anguish is great, but the cost to us as a nation is irretrievable. If we do not move adolescents into responsible adulthood our future is bankrupt.

THE TASKS OF YOUNG ADULTS

Young adulthood, like early childhood, is a time of concern with variations on the themes of self-control and delayed gratification. In fact, the acquisition of self-control and the ability to delay gratification are the pivotal learnings of young adulthood. Once again, self-control is linked to increased choice, and the ability to delay gratification is linked to success in the world. But this time the "pretzel or cookie" choice of early childhood, discussed earlier, is upgraded into choices whose consequences will affect the rest of one's life. In an adult world, self-control is necessary for survival.

Tasks to be completed in young adulthood include

1. getting past the narcissism of adolescence
2. grieving over separation from parents and family
3. finding a job, vocation, or profession
4. setting up a household
5. building intimate relationships, usually choosing a mate and beginning a family
6. recognizing the existence of limits

This agenda is powerful, difficult, complicated, and absolutely essential to adult growth. Only through the avenue of self-control can young adults accomplish these tasks. If they rely on others to do it for them, they will simply delay their entry into adulthood.

Moving beyond the narcissism of adolescence requires young adults to look beyond themselves to others and the world around them. It reminds them they're not the center of the universe. But the struggle to accomplish this task is made far more difficult by our continued romance with permissive self-indulgence. How can we expect our young adults to learn a lesson we are so reluctant to take on ourselves?

In leaving adolescence, young adults must also acknowledge their separation from the family and especially from the position of being a child. If they try to avoid the pain and loss of separation, they'll never feel released from the past. Entering the adult world of increased self-control means relying on oneself to respond to the rules of life. There are no longer persons at hand who will rescue them from life's uncertainties or calamities. Much as they may have wanted to be in charge as adolescents, the reality of adulthood represents the experience of being alone, on their own, without having others to rely on for regulation. Particularly in today's complicated world, the loss of the parental family for structure and support can be very real for many young adults. They heal those feelings of loss by developing adult skills—finding a job, setting up their own households, marrying, and starting to have children. They take on the *roles* of adulthood, even though they may feel ill-prepared and unready.

At this time, gender differences in the paths young adults take begin to emerge. Sixty years ago, a young woman usually chose to marry, set up a household, have children, and remain a homemaker. A young man went to work and spent his energy on the job. He relied on his wife to take care of the home. In more recent years, a woman's choice has become more complicated. Some young women still follow the traditional path of homemaking and mothering. But the majority now enter the work force first for a few years. Later they'll marry and have children, but they'll plan to return to the work force as soon as possible. Regardless of how emancipated they've become, they will struggle to find success in the world of work *and* the world at home.

For a while people believed women could do it all. They were expected to manage the demands of both work and home, and their success was measured on that ability. The trouble was that the job at home frequently required at least as much time as the job at work. The result was that the demands of neither job could be satisfied. Also the requirements of two, full-time jobs generally eliminated the possibility for any leisure, creativity, spirituality, intimacy, or escape for these women. There simply wasn't enough time and energy. Without the balance of these "nonwork" activities, the careful juggling act collapses. Women become burned out, unable to use their gifts for intimacy and spirituality. Children suffer the loss of mothering. The family becomes at risk.

Another complication for young adults has been an economic bind in this country that seems to require both partners to work to support their household. Young adults who've experienced a high degree of economic freedom as children are often reluctant to settle for a significantly lower standard of living as they enter the job market. Similarly two single people holding well-paid jobs may not want to settle for the income of one paid person in a marriage. The solution has been two incomes to support the household and some kind of nonparental care for any children in the family.

But this solution is not without significant problems. Young children have to have safety, protection, and love if they are to survive. Two parents with paid, full-time jobs cannot possibly meet these needs. Solutions such as shared parenting and shared jobs represent major steps toward the resolution of this problem. But not all jobs can be handled that way, and these are not possible solutions for the single parent.

The development of close, intimate relationships is one of the most complicated tasks of young adulthood. If young adults dare not take the risk of intimacy, they'll remain fixated on themselves, never able to experience the miracle and mystery of love. Self-control and the ability to delay gratification are major factors in developing such intimacy. In spite of current admonitions to "let all our feelings out no matter what," intimacy demands a balance between the needs of two people. If I have to have what I want when I want it, I can never be successfully involved in an intimate relationship with another person. If we look to television to define intimacy, we see relationships that are too often chaotic, out of control, and dehumanizing. Where will our children and young adults find a model of intimacy that is worth pursuing?

Unfortunately, we, as adults, have not given young people a very accurate picture of intimacy to use as a model for their relationships. For one thing we haven't talked about the *work* of intimacy. To be really close to another human being requires us to spend time with that person, both in pleasurable activities and in the more difficult times of working through issues that are troubling to the relationship. If our children don't experience intimate contact within the family, they'll miss the opportunity for that firsthand experience of closeness that forms the basis for handling future relationships. Later, when their intimate relationships become threatened by conflict, they won't have the tools for resolution. Their only alternative may be to end a relationship.

In the solving of these problems, young adults are forced to acknowledge the existence of limits and the need to make choices. If they cannot acknowledge limits, they'll find themselves in a world without the freedom of choice. No one likes to experience limitations. Like children in a toy store, we all want to have it all. But in this complex time of young adulthood, critical choices have to be made. The narcissistic presumption that "you can do what you want" must be replaced with the shared reality of "we're in this together" and the awareness that "it may not be possible to have it all." Adulthood requires us to recognize the existence of limits not as inhibitors of freedom but as guarantors of choice. The ability to set limits is directly connected to the capacity for self-control. Without self-control, there is no choice. People out of control have no access to choice; because they feel compelled by their own desires and emotions, their freedom is restricted or removed. Similarly, a nation out of control can no longer protect its citizens from chaos.

The lessons of self-control, delaying gratification, recognizing limits, and making choices are direct routes to adulthood. Learning these lessons virtually guarantees success in all phases of adult life. The learning is quite specific: I can wait; I can choose; I can think; I can plan. I am not driven by my needs or my fears. I understand I am totally responsible for the consequences of my actions.

WHAT NEEDS TO BE DONE

Young adulthood is a difficult time at best, made more difficult by all the changes of the last sixty years. Key growth issues of control and the acceptance of limits do not seem to be valued in American society today. We've become extremely lenient in regard to the free expression of feelings, wants, and needs. If I feel it, I should show it; if I want it, I must have it. If I need it, I'll go to any length to get it. How can we expect young adults to learn that the exercise of self-control always creates choice, if we do not support the concept ourselves? How can we insist they honor any kind of limitations in their behaviors if we continue to indulge ourselves with no regard for others? If we're trying to say to adolescents, "Do as I say, not as I do," we're making a serious miscalculation. Adolescents are far too wise to let us get away with that kind of dishonesty.

Adolescents who are becoming young adults need to see living proof that adults can practice what they preach. They need to know that we won't talk out of both sides of our mouths. If we're going to help them to achieve a reasonably healthy adulthood, we must demonstrate that we are committed to a lifestyle that includes self-control and respect toward others. We have to show them that all the benefits of adulthood are available to them to the extent that they are able to exercise self-control. We have to help them discover the paradox that real freedom depends on our capacity to exercise self-control. We owe them nothing less than our commitment to our own growth as adults and the demonstration of our responsibility to others.

The tasks of adult growth are familiar ones. We've been through them once before, and they feel like old friends. The learning of self-control, the development of survival skills, the assumption of responsibility for others, and the reality of separation and loss are tasks we first encountered in childhood and adolescence, which are now reworked during our adult years. They come in different sizes, shapes, and colors, but they remain steadfastly the same tasks. Our entire lifespan is geared toward learning and growing. That is how we are shaped and refined into the fullest measure of being human.

Young adults need our encouragement and support while they struggle to leave adolescence and face the reality of the additional lessons of adulthood. The work of growth continues throughout our lives. They need a complete picture of adult life that includes struggle, work, success, pain, joy, love, knowledge, loss, acceptance, and the ultimate wisdom of spiritual growth.

As we move through the ongoing process of adult living, with its emphasis on repeated themes, our experience is deepened and intensified. As we repeat these growth experiences at different stages of life, we're given the opportunity to engage in each of them more fully. Like skiers descending a mountain, we cross back and forth from task to task, with widening paths of knowledge, until the journey is finally accomplished.

11

About Middle Adults

In the middle of our adult years, ages thirty-five through fifty-five approximately, we face a double burden of high productivity and maximum responsibility. If there is an overburdened group in the human family, it is that population of middle adults who struggle each day to keep up with too much to do and too little time. "Survival" is their middle name. Middle adulthood revisits latency, the middle period between young childhood and adolescence, redefines and deepens the lessons learned at that time. The issues of this new version of latency are

1. increasing mastery, knowledge, and productivity
2. recognizing that we are not in control of life
3. balancing responsibilities
4. recognizing our dual needs for competency and companionship

INCREASING MASTERY AND RELINQUISHING CONTROL

As our original latency period was a time of maximum learning in childhood, so will these middle adult years represent a time of increased knowledge, mastery, and productivity. Our curiosity and thirst for knowledge will urge us toward greater efforts. We'll move from being skilled to being highly skilled. We'll sharpen our professional abilities. We'll also become more accomplished in the tasks of living outside our work, in our home and the community. We may not be aware of all the knowledge and skill we're acquiring until we look back and can see their accumulation reflected in our greater productivity and achievements.

Paradoxically, in the midst of these positive experiences, we also must face a critical lesson of adulthood, a lesson we'll struggle with many times throughout our lives. We have to come to terms with the fact that life is a process over which we have minimal control. It has its own rhythm and timing, and all our efforts to speed up or delay this process, or bend it to suit our needs, usually interfere with it. We have to learn to let go of our struggle to control life and let it unfold by itself. This is a particularly hard lesson because we've been struggling to gain self-control, and now we must learn to discern the difference between control over ourselves and control over life. It's equally difficult to accept at a time when we're having to be highly responsible in a variety of situations and relationships.

As we go through our adult years, the problem of our lack of control over life will continue to haunt and frustrate us. We'll fight it, flee from it, deny it. We'll keep very busy trying to convince ourselves we're in charge. But in the end its truth is unavoidable. Life will demonstrate this reality in countless ways and experiences. But we won't trust this information until we recognize the futility of our efforts and let go of our insistence that life be lived according to our plan. Ultimately, as life bends and shapes us, we may come to understand that life is fundamentally a spiritual process designed to direct us toward greater understanding and wisdom. Our job is to engage in the process, not try to control it.

BALANCING RESPONSIBILITIES AND NEEDS

In these middle adult years, we also find ourselves struggling to maintain some kind of balance in our lives. The world seems full of too many jobs and too many responsibilities. On every side are demands for time and commitment. One of the hardest parts of this particular time of life is the awareness of, and ambivalence toward, competing needs and responsibilities. We feel responsibilities to our spouse, children, job, self, extended family, friends, church, community, and any volunteer organization we belong to. Life becomes a frustrating juggling act with not enough time for anything.

Our survival depends on how we balance these competing loyalties and pressures. Many times we attempt to settle the dilemma by trying to do it all in order to avoid the tension of having to choose. But the consequence of that behavior is increased stress and frustration, with little satisfaction.

In fact, one of the most significant things we've learned about middle adulthood is the increasing ambivalence people are feeling about their lives and responsibilities.

1. Women who work are questioning whether they can indeed have a successful marriage *and* a successful career *and* healthy children.
2. Women who stay at home question whether they've lost an irretrievable time in their career lives by not working outside the home.
3. Men are questioning whether they want to be caught in the corporate rat race, which allows them little time for marriage and family.
4. Many couples question whether they should have children at all.
5. Some couples are choosing to live together without marrying, thereby reducing their commitment and responsibility to each other.
6. Individuals are opting out of volunteer and community activities because of time pressures and lack of interest.
7. Some people are looking at alternative ways of survival as a way to end their frustration of too many demands and too little time.

People are questioning the *quality* of their life in terms of the *quantity* of demands on their time. Couples are finding themselves living parallel lives with no time for pleasure or intimacy in their relationship. The high divorce rate in this age group is a symbol of the frustration and ambivalence people are experiencing and their painful attempts to make themselves feel better.

Part of the problem stems from our almost desperate need for some relief from the burdens we're carrying. The other part of the problem has to do with society's insistence that the model for life is material success. In today's world most of us do not define success in terms of living, growing, learning, being intimate, and caring for others. Instead, success is usually defined in economic terms. These middle adult years are clearly the time when economic success is at its zenith in importance. If one falters on the success ladder at this stage, one is not likely to be given a second chance. We feel some urgency to perform well, not because we recognize that life is finite but because we feel the hot breath of competitors on our neck. We know we have to keep moving, or they'll overtake us. But the cost to ourselves and those around us is very high.

These middle years are times of hard work and responsibility. But they must also contain opportunities for intimacy and companionship, lightness and play, inner reflection and solitude. As noted in the latency experience, we have dual needs for competency and companionship. When we are under such pressure for success, it's very hard to take care of both of these needs.

The bulk of our experience as parents is spent during these middle adult years. Usually our children are in their own latency experience, and they are particularly vulnerable to the loss of actual time parents spend with them. Their sense of self-worth depends on our valuing them enough to spend time with them. We do them great harm by putting them off because we're too busy. Time put off does not return. What we postpone will most likely never take place. Nowhere is that more apparent than in the family.

We also have very little time for intimacy with ourselves. We play hard, trying to stay in shape, and lose all sense of the pleasure of spontaneous play. We're desperate to relax but find little pleasure even in expensive vacations. We don't know where to go or what to do to find that which we sense is missing in our lives.

THE CRISIS AT FORTY

The mid-life crisis, at forty, described so frequently as a crisis of time, in the sense that life is half over, is more accurately a reflection of the frustration and ambivalence so many middle adults feel. The crisis acts as a catalyst, forcing us to take some kind of action to relieve the intensity of our feelings. People leave jobs, hoping a new position will relieve some of their stress and anxiety. Couples divorce, hoping a new relationship will solve the problem of intimacy in a world that is running too fast and too hard. We're deeply unhappy and hope some action will make us feel better.

In fact, as long as we're trapped in a belief system that counts economic success as the most valued form of achievement, there's little we can do to make ourselves feel better. We seem to have settled for power and success, with companionship and intimacy running a not very close second. The result of that decision is usually ongoing stress, ambivalence, frustration, and a kind of hopelessness that we can change anything. Without the experiences of companionship and closeness, we're a system out of balance, like trying to drive a car with only two wheels. We go nowhere and are incredibly frustrated.

Until we reorganize our values, these middle adult years will continue to be a time of frustration and dissatisfaction. Our insistence on success in the marketplace has become too costly to family life and to personal well-being. The question, Is this all there is to life? reflects the frustration and pain of having too much to do, too little time to do it, and no apparent answers.

No one is in a better place to make significant changes than middle adults. The transition into adulthood has been accomplished; the final years of life are yet to come. And the levels of frustration and dissatisfaction are usually high enough to force us to consider alternative actions. If personal frustration isn't enough to drive us to put our lives more in balance, then we often experience some problem with our physical or emotional health as an indicator that something is wrong. Stress, tension, anxiety, depression, dis-ease of any kind, all call for change in the way we're living our lives.

As we approach the end of the middle adult years, the struggle to learn to let go of our control over life will become even more insistent. Learning to let life unfold becomes more difficult as one sees the beginning of the downhill side of life. There's a tendency to want to have it all, while there's still time.

THE CRISIS AT FIFTY

The crisis at age fifty announces the beginning of the end of this middle period of adult life. It's a different crisis from the mid-life crisis we faced at forty. The problems are unique to this life passage, and the intensity of the experience is unsettling. Fifty has always seemed really "old" to most people during their growing years.

When fifty approaches, we look at it with dismay and disbelief! How did it get here so fast? What happened? We can't believe it—Me, fifty? It doesn't seem possible. But when we get there, fifty doesn't seem quite so old anymore.

We don't look "old," but our inner, child self continues to remember that fifty was once considered pretty ancient. We don't feel different, but we start to sense the winds of change and the beginning of a shift toward the next phase of our adult life. The potency and productivity of these middle years continue. Yet there is a hint of our fragility and vulnerability. Fifty is undeniably past the halfway mark in our life, and there's no way to ignore that truth. But it's confusing when our external lives seem to continue on, business as usual, while our inner lives begin to whisper of change. There is a dissonance and unreality to the whole experience.

Much as we may desire the continuation of life according to our plans, nevertheless, at about fifty, we experience the onset of the aging process. For some, reaching fifty calls forth a renewed effort to stave off aging. We try to deny it by our continued potency at work, by actively exercising, and by attempting to keep up with younger competition. For others, fifty is the beginning of the end, and they start preparing to die.

For most of us, fifty is a unique experience of change. What we could deny before we must now recognize as fact. It may take us several years to absorb the reality. We experience a new vulnerability in this period of time. Most of our major adult decisions have brought us to this place, and each of our previous developmental phases has ended by pointing us into the future. This new shift faces us in two directions. For the first time we will look both forward and backward.

How we *have* lived becomes as important as how we *will* live. Did we strike a balance between conflicting needs? Were we able to give enough time to people we cared about? Did we do enough? Did we make the right choices? If we had it to do over again, would we do it differently? Or we say to ourselves in a more frantic way that time is limited and we'd better change quickly before it's too late.

Throughout our fifties, we have a continuing dialogue between our outer and inner selves. Our outer self goes on flexing its muscles while our inner self begins to express the change that lies ahead. The pressure of this inner self increases. These middle years have been so outwardly productive that there has been little time for us to listen

he reality of one's actual age. Many healthy older people
 they may be chronologically old, but in spirit they're
e's no denying the reality of aging when one approaches
ur inner self, or spirit, long silenced by the burden of
ponsibilities, is just beginning to become more available
 younger than our bodies, almost ageless in its wisdom.
ms to account for the discrepancy we feel between our
ological age and our inner, spiritual age, a discrepancy
with this new phase of our development and continues
f our lives.

 concerns begin to accumulate:

n from parents who have died
n from children who have grown and left home
n from one's job through forced or voluntary retirement
n from the illusion of our immortality
n from friends or spouse who has died
n from life itself

re have we so seriously contemplated the end of life.
us it was always too far in the future to consider. Now it
e for comfort. Try as we may to push thoughts of death
ve a life of their own and slip quietly into our conscious-
vanted clouds on a sun-filled day.
ready to deal with this, we protest. So we try to stave it
e not to retire. We take on additional responsibilities at
the community. We work harder at staying healthy.
ing wrong with any of these efforts, except when they
ial of the issues we have to face in this new time of

scents, we may experience another wave of narcissism,
 our efforts on our health or becoming obsessed with
nd any changes we see happening to them. Or we may
rs and anxieties with a false bravado of indifference or
rn. Time may be passing, but we're in charge of our
We've plenty of time to do what we want!
istent thoughts of death will not be stilled. No matter
 to stop the future, we're into a new place in our
 Our resistance and anxiety are familiar and normal
n unknown future. As our adolescents were ambivalent

to our inner voice. But because we're constructed, as human beings, with a tendency toward balance and health, our inner self now begins to speak loudly enough for us to have to pay attention.

Its insistent message is that we must shift from our attempts to control life to a new awareness of the spiritual nature of our being. What has been rational, dogmatic, and productive in us must give way to the irrational, mysterious, and uncontrollable. Naturally, we seem to have to resist and try to postpone what is "naturally" unfolding both within and without us.

The tempo heightens; the struggle intensifies as we down shift into the next period of life. Our inner self has become intensely audible, asking us about the spiritual quality of our life. Our outer self continues to press us forward. When we allow ourselves to *feel* what is happening, we experience a profound panorama of questions and few, if any, answers. What-has-been has already taken place. What-will-be is unknown. What-it-all-means is to be discovered.

We've had to traverse two major crisis periods (at forty and at fifty) in our middle adult years. We've barely finished with them before we have to move on to the next phase of our adulthood. It's no wonder this transition into the next phase of life feels unsettled and chaotic.

As we enter older adulthood, we encounter a new world that seems more threatening than all the others. We perceive the presence of that which feels utterly inimical to our being. Our death, which had seemed so remote and unreal, now takes on a reality that we can no longer avoid. Because we must contemplate the end of our life, we're also forced to examine the fact of our life. Questions, concerns, fears, despair, surround us like predators in the night, while we face the ultimate limitation of our existence. It is truly a crisis of the spirit.

1

About O

Older adulthood spans the ag
proximately. As we've seen in
rooted in an earlier growth t
adulthood parallel those we sav
has a similar intensity and fe
knowing one is facing the rei
beginning of life. Unlike the
sense of time, the older adul
end.

A SENSE (

When one reaches the mid-fif
the moment and starts anoth
feeling, which starts quietly a
and intensity, is an uneasines
the passage of time. The knov
give way to the anxiety and c
future are couched in not I
There's a sense that many cha
In addition, there's a disc

having and
will tell yo
young. The
sixty. But
too many re
to us. It fee
This fact se
outer, chro
that begins
for the rest
Separatic

▷ separatic
▷ separatic
▷ separatic
▷ separatic
▷ separatic
▷ separatic

Never be
For most of
feels too clo
away, they h
ness like un
We're not
off. We deci
work or in
There's nol
reflect a de
separations.
Like adol
concentratin
our bodies a
cover our fe
lack of conc
lives, we say
But the in
what we do
developmen
reactions to

about leaving childhood and the protective environment of the home, we are equally anxious about moving into the next phase of our development. We've never been there before; we don't know what it will be like. But we sense it will be different from all the phases before it *because* we've become so aware of the limited nature of time.

Much of what we see in these older adult years is a disturbing reminder of change. We notice the gradual diminishing of our powers. Our professional competence is challenged by competitors. Our abilities to take on any task are interfered with by the realities of aging. We get tired; we don't concentrate as easily for as long; our muscles don't work in quite the same way.

There appears to be a quickening of time, perhaps exacerbated by the intensity of our responses. Having earned our maturity and wisdom through years of strenuous effort, we'd like to enjoy the fruits of our labor, rest on our laurels, and hear a congratulatory "well done" by some unseen audience around us. We'd like finally to stop and "smell the roses." Surely we've earned this privilege after surviving all those years of effort. Yet we're into the next period before we've had even a few moments of respite. As in all transitions into the future, we carry an uncertainty and anxiety that manifests itself in a variety of ways.

Our feelings become more intense and more available to us. We don't hide them quite so much under a rational cover, yet we worry that this exposure demonstrates some kind of future instability or senility. We don't take time so much for granted, recognizing the unreliability of the future. We question our lives even more seriously, asking ourselves why we did what we did or whether we should have done differently.

Initially, these questions may be very painful. They're raised in the midst of our knowing that there's nothing we can do to change the past. Gradually, they either become reorganized and accepted or they become persistent reminders of mistakes and wrong turns. They must be worked through over and over until we're released from their power.

If we have children, we watch them become involved in their own lives, with minimal time available for us. This is their time of ascendancy, and because we still live in a world that insists on successful productivity, they'll be caught in the same trap of conflicting demands for their time that we were. Intellectually we can understand what's happening. But the remnants of our own narcissism return to make this attitude of our children feel like another loss. We used to be pretty important to our children. We wonder what's happened. Don't they care about us any more?

That question leads to the more painful questions of aging. What will happen to me? Who will care for me if I am in need? Will anyone be concerned enough to help? We are haunted by pictures of lonely, older people. That fear raises another one. Have I enough economic resources to protect me? Will there be enough money to manage my remaining years or will I be dependent on my children to support me? These feelings of vulnerability and dependence are the same painful fears we faced in our adolescent years. What will come of me? Will I make it? Can I survive?

It's strange suddenly to experience such feelings of fragility after we have completed so many tasks and faced so many problems successfully. We're confused by our indecision and lack of confidence. We're frightened by our uncertainty. We're somewhat ashamed of our emotional reactions to things that didn't stir us before.

A TIME OF TRANSITION

Only when we define this period as a transitional time do we find relief. Indeed, this transition may be the most difficult one we will have to face. At the peak of our power we must once again become novices, struggling to learn the rules of this new stage of life. Yet in this particular beginning, the shadow of death dances around us, beckoning us beyond life to a future that is entirely unknown.

At fifty we could look at both the past and the still assured future. At sixty the future is less certain. The obligation to be productive and responsible to others begins to diminish. The obligation to ourselves becomes more visible.

Some of us discover the special joy of having grandchildren. They may delight and amaze us with their charm or precocity. Once again, as when we were parents, we are the recipients of that special love and affection that children alone can offer to those wise persons who spend time in the care and feeding of the young. Unstructured and uncluttered by outside demands, we find new life and purpose in the special moments between us. Our grandchildren are the promise of tomorrow, but they're also reminders of the present. Being old enough to have grandchildren is a blatant sign of the passage of time. We are undeniably aging.

Back and forth we move, between obligations to others and obligations to ourselves—like dancers moving from one side of the stage to the other. The music compels us to move; the familiar melodies are etched into some part in our brain that automatically responds when we hear the signal. But new and unfamiliar music causes us the anxiety and discomfort of learning new rhythms and movements. It is difficult to learn a brand new dance.

Transitions are like that. It's hard to leave the old dance. We've learned it so well we no longer have to think about how to signal our muscles. Each complicated movement has been learned to perfection. But this new dance requires long hours of hard work. It doesn't feel right; we haven't mastered the movements; we don't feel the automatic connection between brain and body. We wonder if this new dance will ever become so connected to us that we'll welcome the sound of its music.

As we move through this transitional time and into our sixties, the task of accepting our lack of control over life becomes more insistently raised. We first experienced it in our middle adult years as an awareness and frustration that no matter what we did, we simply couldn't control much of what happens in our lives. Jobs change or are lost; friends leave; sickness happens; disasters occur in spite of all our efforts to be responsible and wise.

In the middle years, we saw such events as unwanted intruders, causing us pain and anguish. They assaulted us like an enemy that strikes our weakest defense. All we could do then was resist, heal our wounds, and assemble all our forces to strike back. In our sixties we begin to see a different picture. The out-of-out-control experiences have taken on a new meaning for us as we see that they are connected to the aging process. Now we can no longer deny the forces of change or pretend we're in control and can stop them. We can see the physical changes in our bodies and feel their impact on our lives. Our body, our brain, and our spirit all attest to this new reality. What had been an intellectual construct in our fifties becomes a realized and felt actuality in our sixties. We have no control over the passage of time.

The resistance we feel to our helplessness has deep roots. In their earliest years, children fight to gain some control over their environment and the people in it. Even in the first hours of life, infants let the world know through their cries of protest that they need care and attention. In each progressive state of development, children struggle to be in charge of their lives. We ourselves probably fought our parents continuously over the issue of control. We had the illusion that when we finally left home we'd be fully in charge. Now life has shown us the paradoxical truth. All our struggles to be in control have been illusions. At the zenith of our power, we're once again like children learning the limitations our our power.

In our sixties, the process of life becomes much more visible and palpable. We've come to a vantage point that gives us a mountain-top picture of the path we've traversed. We can see the winding way we've taken. The trail that seemed so uncertain we now view in its totality and predictability. A sort of telescopic lens allows us to zero in on particular moments. We see with a clarity that allows us finally to say, "Of course, that's what was going on. Now I know what that meant. Why didn't I see that before? If I had known then what I know now . . ." Our vision gives us permission really to see and understand. We've entered a new time of possibility characterized by faith.

A TIME OF FAITH

If we're not in control of our lives, then what is? If all our efforts to take charge have no effect on the world around us, then what does? Is there any rhyme or reason to life? Are we predestined to take a certain path and not another? Are we marionettes on a string manipulated by an unseen power? Or do we simply live, grow old, and die? Is that all there is? If we're not in control, why couldn't we have been told that in the beginning and saved ourselves all this pain and suffering? What's it all about anyway?

Wisdom begins when we comprehend that all of life is a process. We're actors in the play, participants on the team. We've been given the gift of life, and our job is to live it as it unfolds before us. As we go through the experiences of living, we're drawn along a path that calls us to act and respond.

It's only through the passage of time that we come to know the paradoxes that life presents to us. Good actions sometimes turn out to have bad consequences. Bad decisions may turn out to be blessings in disguise. What we thought was right may turn out to be wrong. What we experienced as tragic may turn out to be a change for the better. We don't have the vision to know, yet we are called upon to act in spite of our blindness.

Whatever happens to us, even when we encounter life's most difficult situations, is ultimately an opportunity for growth and understanding. We'll fight and resist this explanation. We'll cry out to some unknown perpetrator, "Why did this have to happen?" We'll hate the pain life sometimes inflicts on us with such apparently random and senseless injustice. Why should something as precious as life have to be so difficult?

Perhaps for the first time, a quiet inner voice, the voice of our spirit, will remind us, "Take one day at a time. Wait and see. Don't struggle so hard against what's happening. Try to move with and through the pain to see what's beyond it." That voice helps us see the futility of our efforts at control. Our spirit shows us the wisdom we've earned. Everything we've experienced has brought us to this point in time. *Knowing that we cannot know but must act on faith* is the ultimate truth we've lived to discover. Such wisdom is the result of the effort of living. We learn this lesson through the hard work of being. It's available to everyone, regardless of any limitations we may have, or think we have, by the choice we make to live!

We must make this connection with our spirit, or we'll come to a place of despair. If we cannot accept that we live out our lives, knowing that we cannot know but still must act, we'll continuously revisit the past with recriminations and misery. Life will not be worth living if we believe *we* could have changed it, *we* should have done differently, *we're* culpable, and it's too late.

Until the very moment of our death, this connection is available to us. We're drawn to this water of wisdom many times; but it is we who must drink at this well and be transformed by its healing water. No one else can do it for us.

Reaching a point where we can lay down our arms and embrace life, with all its complexities, joys, and sorrows, is our crowning victory. It's the message that gives meaning and definition to our lives: to trust without seeing; to know without knowing; to have faith in the midst of our not understanding.

But these words of our spirit are available to us only after we've fought to control life and discovered how meaningless our efforts are. These words speak to our limitations and vulnerabilities; they assure us that our struggle to survive has not been in vain.

As we approach the end of our sixties, we have traversed the main thoroughfares of our lives. Most of us have raised our children. We have probably retired from the jobs that supported us. The struggle to be productive is no longer the focal point of our lives. We have left behind the world's measurement of success. The separations we've experienced have taught us hard lessons about the real meaning of life. We are entering a new phase of life in which we'll gain our final glimpse of the meaning of life, which transcends all our human efforts, ambitions, and pride. Aging in body but young in spirit and gaining in wisdom, we approach the years of old age with an increased awareness of final tasks and questions. How will we live? How shall we die? What can we leave behind that will give us a measure of immortality?

13

About Adults in Old Age

Old age encompasses the years from seventy until the end of our lives. Although we must still deal with the basic tasks that have continued from earlier stages in life, the distinguishing task of old age is the acceptance of life and the recognition that life has meaning. The work of old age is essentially spiritual, and it is as necessary to our well-being as any other work we've accomplished in the process of living.

BASIC CONCERNS

After we've crossed the difficult threshold into old age, we once again look around for familiar bench marks. We are still concerned with self-control, survival, and separation but in a different form. Rather than falling neatly into distinct categories, these themes interplay and weave around one another like a melodic line with various counter melodies.

Self-control becomes linked with health concerns. Most of us in old age will say that health becomes the major determinant of our attitude toward life. If we're in reasonably good health, life continues to feel productive and possible. But if our health is noticeably declining, it becomes the focus of our attention.

Self-control is also related to changes in our bodies. We used to take our bodies for granted. Whatever might go wrong was only a temporary phenomenon that would return to a normal state whenever we got around to doing something about it. Now our bodies tell us in one way or another that some changes are irreversible.

Part of the task of self-control is to learn to accept these changes and to maintain some degree of equanimity around this process of aging. We can and must observe the rules of good health. But we must also learn that there are limits to our control over our bodies. Nowhere is this more directly observable than during the aging process.

Intermixed with our concern about self-control is our concern about survival. Our major responsibilities toward others have decreased. Our current task is to be as responsible for ourselves as we can. The interplay between these themes is obvious. We can survive more effectively if our health continues to remain good. We can continue to deal responsibly with life if we retain reasonably good self-control.

As we loosen our ties of responsibility to others, we're faced with additional, painful questions. Am I of *any* use to anyone else? If I'm not actively engaged in caring for others, will I be alone? How long will I be able to be responsible for myself? Will there be enough money for my remaining years? Will some catastrophic illness or disaster wipe out my financial security? Will my children take care of me if I need them? Will all my work of responsibility toward others be repaid in kind?

Earlier in life we were always able to quiet our fear about survival through our productive efforts. As long as we could support ourselves financially and be responsible for others, we could escape the fundamental and terrifying question of our own survival: If I couldn't care for myself, would there be anyone there to take care of me?

Intimately connected to our concerns about survival are the continuing losses in the separations we experience. These separations now focus on our being alone and our dying. What will it be like to die? Will I be alone? Will I suffer? Is there anything after this life?

These questions become very basic to us. Like food, clothing, and shelter, they represent fundamental concerns that demand our attention. But if they become our *only* concerns, these final years of life will become painful experiences of panic and fear.

THE LIFE OF THE SPIRIT

The most reliable antidote for this fear is the development of our spiritual life and the recognition that this work is the final task to be undertaken in our life cycle. Fear can yield to faith when we begin to concentrate on this new task at hand. Without the experience of acceptance and faith, we'll leave this life fighting and struggling against that which has never been opposed to us, shadow boxing in the darkness against an enemy that doesn't exist.

In these years everything is focused on our being able to learn this lesson of acceptance and faith. There are no crises to distract us at the end of each decade. To become seventy is like becoming eighty or ninety. We pass through these "life locks" with open gates and flowing waters. We have neither to take charge of nor to control anything or anyone else. We have time to devote to the growth of our spirit. We still have sufficient energy and resources to listen to our inner voice. We have the vision to see long distances in the past. We have the wisdom to know that we cannot know the future, yet we must continue to live.

It remains for us to loosen our grasp on control in any form. We must become trustworthy messengers of the meaning of life, hiding nothing and holding nothing back. We must live life as a pure process that moves us toward deeper wisdom and connection to God.

If we have faith, we understand that life is a continuous call to live in relationship with God. The years of old age allow us to focus exclusively in that direction. But we can do that only if we're willing to accept the gift of life we've been given to live, not what-might-have-been, but what-actually-was. Dwelling on what-might-have-been will only tie us in knots of unrelieved pain. Thinking "If only . . ." will drown us in the anguish of regrets. If we indulge ourselves in recriminations over mistakes made, wrong turns taken, we will obsessively compile a list of "war crimes" we've committed for which we see no forgiveness or repatriation.

There can be no peaceful coexistence between our physical selves and our spiritual lives until we can accept the miraculous gift of life, which we have lived to the best and sometimes the worst of our ability. Faith is our awareness that we went through the actions of living, however successful or unsuccessful they were, in order to discover the limited nature of life's transactions. In the working out of our spiritual life, we transcend all the ruminating and questioning and turn ourselves toward God.

In the light of faith, the everyday concerns of self-control, survival, and separation are the necessary props and scenery for the play, but the essence of the drama is the interaction between creature and Creator.

In earlier years we were caught in a web of tasks that were all-consuming and at times overwhelming—homes to maintain, children to raise, skills to learn, tasks to do, things to acquire, a living to make. There was always too much to do, and it often seemed unmanageable and out of our control. Will there ever be time for me? Am I doing any of this right? Shouldn't there be more to life than this?

When we reach old age, we let go of many of these tasks. In fact, letting go is always what we must do when we leave one stage and enter a new one. But in this particular transition to old age we must let go of many of the things that have *defined* us—our work, our children, our successes, our control of the world around us. It's not easy. The intensity of our resistance is a testimony to the difficulty of the task.

To overcome our resistance and accept the fact of our aging, we must recognize old age as a time of consolidation, *the linking of our spiritual lives with our everyday living*. We must acknowledge this as a period of culmination and fruition, earned precisely by all our efforts at living. If we regard old age as a time of accumulated wisdom, we must also be willing to grant to old age the respect and admiration it deserves. It merits nothing less.

Unfortunately, in America in the 1990s, we do not look at old age as the reward for the achievement of living. We do not seem to value the wisdom of older people. We do not believe in their visions. We do not savor their knowledge and experience. Instead we seem to want to get rid of them. We pack them into retirement or nursing homes, putting them with their own "kind," telling ourselves they'll feel more comfortable that way. We provide fewer medical services for them, because it's not cost effective. We put some of them on drugs, hoping it will keep them moderately sedated and out of trouble. We don't seem to want to be bothered.

In treating the elderly as we do we've lost all the gifts they have to give us. The loss of respect for old age cuts us off from our heritage and traditions. We become a flat universe, a two-generational family with only the present available to us. That which connects us to our history is lost. The multi-dimensionality of life slips away, and we become fixed in the now, having continuously to relearn the lessons of the past.

Much as we cannot afford to shortchange our children's growth, we also dare not lose the wisdom and spirituality of our older population. In fact, how we treat our oldest citizens is a clear picture of how we view life itself.

If life does not gain in meaning, then why live? If all we have to look forward to after the struggle of living is an unvalued, second-class status, then what has it all been about? If our final days are to be spent in destitution, where is the mystery and wonder of the gift of life?

In the last few years, psychologists have begun to look at three-generational families, including children, parents, and grandparents. Therapeutic interventions have included meetings with all three generations, with tasks being assigned to each. Repeated patterns are visible and fascinating reminders of our historical interconnectedness and interdependence. Part of the task of old age is becoming aware of the invisible ties that bind one generation to another through the process of living.

To become consciously spiritual, to be engaged in activities of the spirit, is the pathway we've waited all our lives to take. Achievements disappear into actions of kindness. Striving for future success yields to living in the moment, breathing in the wonder of being alive. Complexity yields to simplicity. The attempt to control life is transformed into the acceptance of what we do not know.

Our eyes now see that which we were formerly too busy to see. Our ears hear sounds that we never noticed before. The world looks different when viewed through spiritual lenses. Both the beauty and the ugliness are more apparent to us, like experiences of light and dark stripped of their defensive covers. Each is part of the experience called living.

THE END AND THE BEGINNING

In these final years we discover that the end of life is linked to the beginning of life in an amazing circle. As our death was a reality from the moment we were born, so too as we approach death we become reconnected to the source and beginning of life. In our old age, we're sometimes like children, full of a sense of wonder and mystery of life yet also fragile and vulnerable, needing comfort, care, and love. At the same time, as the end of life comes closer, our fears of dying take us out of the realm of childhood. We no longer enjoy the innocence of not knowing.

We've lived with fear before. Our bodies are familiar with the automatic reaction of the fight-or-flight response. We know how disabling fear can be. But the fear of dying is a new kind of fear. In our other fears we could at least look ahead to a time when terror would subside and we would be calmed. This time we can see only a vast unknown. We don't even know what to hope for. We truly know that we cannot know because no one can tell us, with absolute certainty, what's in store for us after we die.

What we do know is that life leads us through a continuous series of growth experiences, each experience shaping and refining us toward the next one. Each shift to a new stage in life means letting go of the previous state of being and embracing the new one. As we move through these stages and states, we gain an increasingly broader perspective, particularly as we're able to link growth experiences together. When we let ourselves learn from our life experience, we also discover that what happens at one stage prepares us for what will occur later.

Death is the end of life as we know it. If the life pattern of successive stages continues to repeat itself, death will be followed by some kind of new beginning, which we cannot know until we arrive at that place.

In accepting the fact of our death, we also accept the paradoxes that are the keys to wisdom: In order to live in a new stage of life, something in us from the previous stage must die. In order to let go of our lives, we must claim their integrity. In order to release ourselves from the struggle of life, we must learn to accept it.

We can accept these paradoxes when we are able to see the meaning of life set within a spiritual framework. When facing death, we can hang on to life even by the smallest of threads, like a terrified novice on a high wire, or we can accept the miracle that we have lived at all, and let go!

If life is a gift, then each moment has been a renewed expression of the generosity of the Giver. If life is truly a birthday present, then the only expression required of us is gratitude. Any other response is unnecessary.

But in being grateful, we must accept the entire gift, not just a selection of the parts we like. In learning to be thankful for all of life, we must finally accept all the things we do not understand or know about life, which is to say, we must learn to trust the Giver of the gift.

In learning to trust, we return to the beginning of life in which we, as infants, first learned to trust. In our helplessness, we relied on our parents for their care and protection. Once again in our old age, we're helpless as we face this new death experience. Our final growth is the trust we give to the One who gave us the gift of life, a trust that allows us to face our death, the ultimate unknown of our existence.

Trust, acceptance, and gratitude are words that take on new meaning in our old age. We now understand them to be truths essential to life and a message we are uniquely able to offer the world. In fact, if we do not proclaim this saving message, these truths will not be heard.

Whatever our spiritual affiliations may be, these final years offer us the special opportunity to be grateful and accepting of this amazing gift called life. Our gratitude encompasses the known and the unknown, the wise and the foolish, the easy and difficult experiences of living. All of it is offered to the One who gave us the gift. Our task was to accept the gift of life and live it. In our final moments all that is left is to trust and let go!

14

Summaries and Connections

Part 1 described the family as buffeted by societal changes that have caused major ruptures in its traditional form. Into that changing social picture of the family are now placed the developmental changes in the individual described in Part 2.

Families are made up of members at different stages in their life development. We traverse these life stages with varying degrees of difficulty and struggle. Someone in the family is always going through some kind of transition that requires understanding and consideration. The family has stood as a shelter along the way, the place where we could stop and rest, in order to continue.

When the family cannot provide these necessary supports, growth is interrupted. If this basic structure of American society, the family, is not able to provide the conditions of growth, it will be almost impossible for society to move from its adolescent preoccupation with self into responsible adulthood. If we cannot become a responsible society, our future is in grave jeopardy. We're entirely interconnected. What happens in society happens to the family. What happens in the family also happens to society. The individual, who is a part of both the family and society, is affected by each and can act on both.

TASKS OF THE INDIVIDUAL

As we go through life, the same themes are repeatedly addressed: self-control, survival (including responsibility and intimacy), and separation. Life gives us endless opportunities to develop these themes in an amazing interplay of experiences, each one offering possibilities of further refinement and redefinition, until they merge finally in old age. These are the psychological tasks that enable us to respond to societal rules and regulations and to live with one another with common understanding and devotion.

We've discovered, however, that each of these psychological tasks becomes transformed into a spiritual task as we continue through the life cycle. Having achieved self-control, we must now recognize how limited our control of life is, which can lead us to yield to God's control. Having become productive and proficient, we must accept the limitations imposed by the aging process and undertake the task of developing spiritual understanding. Having experienced separations from loved ones, we must face our own separation from our families and this life, to reconnect to the Creator, who brought us into this life, thereby completing the life cycle.

We're perfectly constructed to be able to complete both the psychological and spiritual tasks of this lifetime because we're geared toward maintaining a healthy balance. Nevertheless, all the years of our lives we work hard at this business of living, often struggling without sufficient guideposts or assistance. We're continually having to learn new ways of being, suffering the anxiety of constant change and growth.

The timetable of growth differs from person to person. The suggested time frames are approximations clearly subject to individual variations. Some persons achieve spiritual understanding in early adulthood. Others never achieve it. Many of us struggle to achieve a minimum of understanding throughout our lives. Most of us resist life's lessons with varying degrees of determination. We all have a hard time loosening our control over life and allowing life to unfold without our having to be in charge. We are caught in our survival mode, seeing only our need to be responsible, to do it all ourselves.

But it's precisely in the surrender of our control and the acceptance of life's lessons as they unfold that we are transformed into persons of understanding and gratitude.

THE EFFECT OF SOCIETY ON THE FAMILY

That it's tough to live today is an understatement at the very least. Life has become so complex and its circumstances so transient that most of us can scarcely keep up with the pressure to adjust to the changes. We're in a nationwide state of anger, frustration, and burnout as a result of the shifting foundations beneath us and the continuous barrage of demands on us.

Part 1 of this book surveyed the incredible number of societal changes during the last sixty years that have directly affected each of us. Changes have happened everywhere, in the government, in the community, in the church, in the school, in the neighborhood, and most painfully in the one place we needed to stay constant, the family. We've watched the family move from one configuration to another, like a skier descending a treacherous hill, dodging rocks and trees, struggling to stay upright while moving faster and faster as darkness approaches and the descent becomes more dangerous. Confused by change and frightened for our very survival, we need to slow our speed and find a more stable environment, one that will help us see where we need to go and what we need to do.

Earlier chapters have stated that the most significant changes outside the family resulted from a societal shift toward a preoccupation with narcissistic concerns, an obsession with individual happiness and fulfillment. This external shift has been matched within the family by the increasing loss of stabilizing, parenting figures. The consequence is that the family has lost much of its importance as a provider of security, comfort, and training for living in our society. We're now relying on outside agencies—day-care centers, baby-sitters, schools—to provide those essential experiences.

We've become a society of disparate families, with little to hold us together: both parents working, children going in various directions for lessons and care, families who are frantic for time together but can scarcely find time for a common meal. The complexity of our lives has taken away the very essence of our lives, which is the unstructured time we spend together as a family.

THE EFFECTS OF SOCIETY AND THE FAMILY
ON THE INDIVIDUAL

Individual growth has already been altered by the changes in the family and society. As individual growth is disrupted, there will be repeated disturbances in the fabric of society. Children who are not taught the rules and regulations of society grow into adults who break the law. Adults, frustrated and angered by the changes in society, do not provide the kind of parenting that is required by children. They also do not provide a model for adulthood that is worth struggling to achieve. Parents and children who cannot find time to spend in living together miss the very essence of what it means to be a human being. If our humanity is gone, our society is lost.

In each phase of individual development discussed, we've seen the impact of the last sixty years of social change. Young children are struggling to learn basic lessons of self-control in a society that has become largely out of control. Latency-age children are not learning the fundamental tasks and responsibilities of living. Fewer parents are available to teach them, and society no longer seems to place a high value on such basic activities. Adolescents have been particularly affected by societal changes. Our societal narcissism has deeply interfered with their ability to become adult. The fears of young adults about being able to make it in an adult world are fueled by society's insistence that achievement is a matter of economic success.

Middle adults are caught between too many responsibilities and a society that promotes narcissism and economic success, leading a schizoid life with little contentment and happiness. Older adults feel frustration and fear that their life is coming to an end in an unbalanced society that has lost its concern for the greater good in its preoccupation with the individual. The elderly have the time to devote to spiritual growth but live in a society that does not honor or respect them.

As individuals, our developmental experiences have been significantly altered by these changes in our family life and in society. Our families have become reflectors of the chaotic conditions we've endured these last sixty years. Our society is caught in a flood tide of change that feels overwhelming and out of control. The ability to see and understand a spiritual dimension to life has been greatly reduced by the continual crises in both the family and society. We're so busy putting out fires, there's no time to think about anything but our day-to-day survival. If we lose our spiritual connection, we will live out our lives without meaning and purpose.

Our task is to restore order. Because we're so totally interconnected, no one is exempt from the work at hand. As the changes of the last sixty years have accumulated into the present-day crescendo of the cult of individualism, so must we begin the task of family restoration, knowing it will be years before the impact of our work will be felt. The time to begin the work, however, cannot be delayed. The future of the family and our society is at stake.

PART 3

THE FUTURE OF THE FAMILY

15

Divorce and Single Parenting

Divorce has had a profound impact on family life and the future of the family. Prior to the 1960s, divorce was something that happened to very few families. It was not an option for most people. But the painful upheavals of the 1960s disturbed every aspect of life, including the family. For the next two decades a rising divorce rate would overwhelm the family.

As with all societal changes, we didn't realize the enormity of what was happening until much later, when we saw it in retrospect. At first, we were pretty brave about the whole thing. Divorce happens, we said, but we'll all survive. We thought we'd have some difficulty in the beginning, but once the divorce was final the worst would be over. Because we believed that children would be especially harmed by ongoing marital discord, we thought dissolving destructive marriages was acting in the children's best interests. Give or take a few months or years of recovery, things would be normal again. In the early days of divorce, we were brave, simplistic, and almost hopeful in our belief that things would be better once we'd made the break.

For a few years we concentrated on the impact of divorce on the marital partners, especially some of the more practical aspects of divorce. What was it like to be divorced? How do I find my way back into society as a single person? How do we work out the details of visitation and holidays? We knew divorce was a painful experience, but we thought it would become less troublesome as it became more common.

THE PAIN OF DIVORCE

Instead of time relieving the stress and pain of divorce by making it a more normal occurrence, we found quite the opposite. Over time, the pain of divorce became more visible and excruciating rather than less. For most adults, divorce means total change—changes in our social, economic, and community status. Divorce means anger and pain, rejection and loss. Divorce usually means an expensive legal process, which is economically disastrous and emotionally shattering. The impact of divorce is like an endless, repeating loop. Just when we think the cycle is finished, a new experience brings the painful trauma back, playing the same melody but now in a new key.

Even when children are finally grown, the pain returns in a new series of special events that are normal family celebrations but also reminders of the changes in the particular family that has been shattered by divorce. Graduations, marriages, and the arrival of grandchildren are all reminders of the family theme, which continues to play, regardless of the dissonance of divorce. What we thought was an end to an era of sadness and anger turns out to be an ongoing recycling of pain and adjustments.

If there are children in the family, the parental relationship does not die when a divorce occurs. It changes form but continues to exist. We cannot underestimate the biological connection of parenting. In fact, most of us do not divorce ourselves from our children, and we can never destroy the reality that our former spouse was also the co-parent of our children. We cannot annul the fact of the family. Paradoxically, although divorce ruptures marriage and the family, it is also a testimony to the power of these institutions, as evidenced by the large numbers of people who divorce and later remarry their original partners.

As we discovered the full impact of divorce on us as adults, we also began to learn of the cost of divorce to our children. We had hoped that *we* would endure the major pain of divorce, relieving our children of pain, stress, and guilt and allowing them a future less marred by conflict. We were wrong. Rather than feeling guilty about their part in their parents' divorce, children feel sad that their parents have separated. Rather than feeling relieved to have the conflicts in the home lessened, many children wish their parents were still together, no matter what the marital situation was like. Years after the divorce, many grown children still have longings that the marriage had remained intact. The special occasions of adulthood are reminders for them of the family that once was.

Children recognize the power of the family because their dependence permits them to see the necessity for parental care. They want what they need. A great deal of the disruptive behavior they engage in during and after a divorce represents their attempts to hold the family together. Their message to us is simple: "We need you. Look! See how much we need you. We're in trouble so you'll have to stay and help us." Their hope is that if they can make us turn our attention toward them and their needs, we'll have to forget our own plans and needs. Their tenacity and willingness to try almost anything to distract us from our problems are remarkable.

For the most part, their efforts are not successful. We do not see the chaos they create for what it really is. We punish their behavior, not realizing that their efforts are unconsciously directed toward holding us together. *We're* angry and frustrated with them for not seeing how disruptive they are, particularly as our energy to deal with them is so depleted. *They're* frightened and sad, having lost their one chance to turn us around, and they're worried about their future.

In the last ten years, the procedure for obtaining a divorce has become so complicated that the pain is intensified to an almost unbearable degree. Divorce used to take a few months, with a minimum amount of negotiating except in the most complicated situations. Today, it may take two to three years of intense battling to settle marital and property differences.

Throughout this prolonged settlement period, parents and children are subjected not only to the conflicts of their own relationships; they've also become part of a legal system that introduces further antagonism between the marital partners. Lawyers assume adversarial positions that intensify rather than ameliorate the situation. The financial security of the family, already undermined by having to split resources, is further reduced by legal fees. Original grounds for conflict become battle positions, with repeated volleys and growing casualties. The final result is an exhausted cease-fire. The battle weary couple may have won the divorce, but the suffering is not over.

HEALING THROUGH MEDIATION
AND SUPPORT GROUPS

As we have discovered the painful cost to both children and parents in a divorce, we're beginning to look for ways to help families heal after a divorce. We've found that the quality of the postdivorce relationship between marital partners is the key to healing the pain of divorce for the entire family. If the divorce does *not* produce a cessation of conflict and a reduction in pain, then children, in particular, continue to struggle in an impossible situation. Having been unable to stop the divorce in the first place, and now caught in ongoing marital discord and hate, they may give up hope for any future for themselves. If their parents couldn't end the war between themselves, even after a divorce, how can they believe in *their* own chances to succeed in life. If their parents couldn't make it, why will they be any different?

These children are stuck in a web of unresolved conflict. Snared by their parent's inability to settle their differences, they're trapped in between the two people they've needed the most. To turn toward one parent means turning away from the other. Their only strategy may be to remain caught in the middle, stunting their growth in favor of not increasing the conflict. If parents continue to do battle, in obvious or subtle ways, they condemn their children to remain trapped in the parents' conflict. *If for no other reason than their children's health and growth, divorcing partners have to create a climate of resolution between each other after a divorce.*

Marital partners who find ways to bring their conflicts to some kind of resolution create an environment in which everyone can move beyond the divorce. It is now recognized that there is a recovery time of several years before all members of the family can truly resume their lives. But if the postdivorce relationship can become more amicable than inimical, everyone can survive the process.

Divorce mediation seems to be a step in that direction. As a nonbinding attempt to counsel couples about all aspects of divorce, it generally takes place outside the legal system, except when it is mandated by the court. A person trained in divorce mediation can be an invaluable friend to a family by facilitating its passage through the painful settlement process.

We no longer have to hide the fact of our divorce. All kinds of groups have been formed to help single people and single parents. Divorce groups help to normalize the divorce process, providing nonjudgmental help and support through the legal process as well as during the emotional reality of the postdivorce experience. Many schools now provide support groups for children of divorce.

These nonfamilial resources are particularly useful because the extended family is often unable to be helpful during a divorce. Relatives are usually too close to the participants to understand what is happening and often manage to polarize the situation into the villain and victim, taking one side or another in an attempt to do something. It's hard for everyone to realize that in a divorce both parties are part of the conflict, no matter what the situation appears to be. The healing of the pain of a divorce cannot take place until marital partners are both willing to own their contribution, an attitude that permits the relatives to be less rigid in taking sides.

THE SINGLE PARENT AND THE PARENTAL ALLIANCE

The inevitable result of divorce is a growing number of single-parent families. The burden on the single parent to provide all the care, protection, and education for the children is overwhelming. Even if each single parent works conscientiously, there's no backup parent in a one-parent situation. It's like being on duty twenty-four hours a day, seven days a week. Whatever happens, the single parent is fully responsible. Additionally, most single parents have to work in order to offset greatly reduced economic resources. The stress and strain for both the single parent and the children is overwhelming, and family time for anything but the bare essentials becomes almost nonexistent. For many single parents, the aftermath of the divorce may represent an even greater struggle to keep up with the demands of children, home, and a job than the divorce itself was.

One of the most interesting and direct solutions for the near impossible task of the single parent is the concept of the parental alliance. Couples who cannot form a marital alliance may be able to create a parental alliance, consciously working together for the sake and welfare of their children. Couples who can get past the conflicts of their divorce can present their children with a team approach to parenting that provides for their children's needs in the present and offers them hope for their future.

Since it may not be possible to form a parental alliance with one's former spouse, such an alliance could be formed with a grandparent, a baby-sitter, a friend, or another divorced adult. The crucial factor is the assumption of joint responsibility in the raising of the children. Both parties need not live together, but they need to form a commitment to parent together, a commitment that children know about and can rely on.

Obviously such an agreement cannot replace the experience of growing up with two parents who stay together, and such an agreement is not legally binding. But it would be an acknowledgment of a basic principle in family life that has become painfully clear. Children really do need two adult, parenting persons who are committed to their growth and development. The job of parenting is too complicated to be accomplished by one person for a prolonged period of time. Single parents do the job because they have to. But most would agree that the burden is overwhelming and that they would welcome almost any help they could get. The cost for children is not getting what they need for their growth and development and never reaching their full potential as human beings.

RECOGNIZING OUR RESPONSIBILITY

We're finally beginning to understand the great paradox of divorce. As parents, we must work together while in the process of breaking apart. We must create some kind of harmony in the middle of disharmony, make reasonable that which seems unreasonable, in order for children to survive, pick up the pieces of their lives, and continue to grow. If the dissonance continues, their lives will also continue to be disrupted. Too many children lead unnecessarily schizoid lives, bouncing back and forth between battling parents, like a volley ball in a contest of wills, punched and pushed across a net of unfinished anger and pain.

They do their best to satisfy both sides. But because the game doesn't end, they're not free to leave. Clearly we don't have the right to require them to play.

There's a phrase in the traditional marriage ceremony that reads, "till death do us part." Especially in a divorce, this remains most poignantly true. We *are* parents for life. No matter how necessary it is that we disengage from our marriage, we continue to be parents. We retain that role, divorced or married, so that our children may continue their growth and become functioning adults. Their needs must be met, and it is our job to meet them. As parents we can do nothing less. While we may continue to choose to divorce, we cannot divorce ourselves from our responsibility to parent our children.

THE AMBIVALENCE OF DIVORCE

Society is ambivalent about divorce. On the one hand we see it as an assault against the family. We recognize its trauma for the participants, its particular cost to children, and its lifelong impact on the entire family. On the other hand, we also know that not every marriage is "made in heaven." Many marriages should not continue because they are hazardous to the well-being of the marital couple or the family or both. Other marriages do not continue because they cannot stand up to the test of time. Some relationships are destructive and need to end. For some people, divorce is the only option in an unendurable situation that is no longer life-giving. Divorce is then seen as a courageous action to improve their lives.

Most people who divorce are operating out of the belief that life could be better. It is to be hoped that they will find the courage to learn from the experience and the vision to begin again. As in all of life's lessons, what is learned is often in proportion to the depth of the struggle.

Divorce for adults is a time of pain and suffering. But it also contains the potential for great growth. Even for the person who's being divorced against his or her will, the learning is not lost. It may take more time to grieve; the anger and rage may seem endless. But the meaning of the experience will become clearer as life continues to unfold. Not uncommonly, those so-called victims of divorce often turn out to be the ones who gain the most insight from the experience. Their pain becomes a compelling catalyst for change.

In all life's painful struggles, time remains the great healer. Nowhere is that more apparent than in a divorce. It takes a considerable amount of time before the pain begins to ease. But over time, if we can give ourselves to the healing and learning process, we can enter a new place of understanding and growth.

Support groups preach the message of the benefits of time and encourage us to trust in the healing process. That is why they are so helpful to divorced persons and single parents. Those who have already experienced the trauma of divorce and survived are guiding lights of hope for those who still feel trapped in the darkness of their pain and suffering. The survivors share their stories and help the newly divorced see that over time, they'll feel better and finally they'll feel healed.

Because of the intimacy of marriage, judgments about a divorce are difficult to make. We really don't know what goes on in other people's houses. But we do know that divorce must be taken with great seriousness, because we've come to understand its complexity in the present and its lifelong impact on the family.

In our ambivalence about divorce, we have shifted our position about what's best for the children. For a time, as noted, we thought it was better for children not to experience parental conflict. We thought we should never stay together "for the sake of the children." So we ended our combative marriages and tried to build new lives. More recently we've decided children can tolerate marital conflict and in fact often prefer that parents stay married, no matter what.

In our struggle to come to terms with the reality of divorce, there are two provisions we must make. One is that divorce must be available for those situations that require it. Hazardous conditions require action to remove the danger. Relationships that are not life-giving but that cannot be altered may have to be ended. The decision in each case is highly individualized and personal. The other provision is that divorce must not be too easy to obtain. Because we now know the long-range cost to the family, we must include that knowledge in our decision whether or not to divorce. We no longer can claim ignorance. We must take into account the full effect of our actions. Whatever we do, we must provide for our children's continued growth and safety. We cannot abandon them while we struggle with our future. We owe them a chance at their own future.

The challenge is to create an environment in which good will can replace ill will for the sake of everyone in the family, whether that includes divorce or not. The solution must be for better—for everyone.

16

Remarriage and Stepparenting

In spite of the pain and anguish created by a divorce or the death of a spouse, we've not stopped remarrying and trying to form families. We've assigned the name blended families, sometimes called reconstituted families, to those new families that represent the merging of two previously married persons and their children, creating a new category of relationships called stepparents and stepchildren.

Within the newly formed blended family, there are amazing configurations of adults and children. On the adults' side are the wife and possibly her parents, siblings, other relatives, former husband, former in-laws, and their network of relatives; and the husband and possibly his parents, siblings, other relatives, former wife, former in-laws, and their network of relatives. On the children's side there might be natural children, stepchildren, half siblings, and step siblings. Stated more simply, the children in this blended family may be "his," "hers," and possibly "ours."

Complex as it is, this blended family creates a new kind of extended family, which is its potential strength and most life-giving promise. In extending our boundaries to include new family ties, we create the possibility of an unusual network of support and care. If the blended family is to succeed, it will need the strength created by these new relationships as a buttress against all the trauma released in the merging of two families.

PROBLEMS OF REMARRIAGE

The problems for this newly formed family lie primarily in the deeply complicated interrelationships that make up the blended family and the network of extended family that surrounds it. When two people marry who already have children from a former marriage, they will need support, courage, persistence, and love. At the moment they begin their life together, their marriage is statistically destined to fail.

The problems of blended families usually fall into four categories: unfinished business from the previous marriage, an overload of needs in the new marriage, insufficient funds, and insufficient time.

Unfinished Business

Unfinished business from the previous marital and family situation is the opening battleground for the blended family. If a divorce preceded the remarriage, there are likely to be unsettled strains of anger, hurt, resentment, jealousy, and loss. Often the divorce itself is still being acted out over issues of custody, visitation rights, and financial support. If the previous marriage ended in a death, the complications of custody and visitation are absent, but the past is full of memories, dreams, and ways of being that were part of another intimate relationship. In either circumstance, new ways of relating and living will be required if the new family is to survive.

In the beginning it's like an emotional free-for-all just waiting to happen. All the participants seem to be holding their breath, knowing the first "domino" of emotional release will create a chain effect, which will be unstoppable until the last one has fallen. If all the dominoes go down, and all those emotions are released, what will be left of this brave, new blended family?

Over time it becomes obvious that any thought of a blended family living happily ever after, like television's "Brady Bunch," is pure bunk. Every person in a blended family is in a life-and-death struggle to survive. Survival means enduring the loss of a biological parent and the family of origin. Survival means living with a new stepparent and possibly step siblings, whether one wants to or not. Survival means the redefinition of self into a new family. Survival means learning to be married in the middle of a fully formed, highly charged, explosive family environment.

The trouble for many couples in a remarriage is that they are living in the present but are unconscious repeaters of the past. They begin this new relationship with wonderfully good intentions—this time it's going to be different! But in short order, they're so engulfed in the complexity of their new life that they resort to old, familiar ways to relieve the tension and stress.

Children also bring unfinished issues from the previous family to this new one. The loss of a parent through death or divorce is a profound experience. It's usually years before the child can feel the full weight of the loss. At the time, it's too much to bear. The impact of the divorce itself, all the pain leading up to the actual dissolution of the marriage, as well as the postdivorce experience of adjustment are painful experiences that cannot possibly be completely healed by the beginning of a new marriage and family.

The unfinished business from the past lingers on into the present, setting up a situation that is already overloaded when it has just begun. There's seldom time for a honeymoon (real or symbolic) in a remarriage situation. The spector of unfinished business is omnipresent and explosive, like a fire waiting for the match to be lit.

Present Needs

Simultaneously, we're well into the issues and questions of the present. If there's been a divorce, are there custody problems? Which parent is the custodial parent? Whose children are in which house what part of the time? Who has which children for what holidays? Who pays for what expenses? Are these arrangements amicable or an ongoing battle? Literally dozens of issues are worked and reworked as two families with former lives try to bring those lives into the new family.

Beyond these practical matters of who, what, where, when, and why are the more frankly emotional concerns of loss, fear, anger, sadness, and pain. Each parent and child carries with him or her the burden of the "lost family" as he or she tries to engage in this new family. Everyone has his or her own resentments about the intrusion of strangers into the family.

New sibling rivalries occur. Which set of children get the better deal? Are her children always treated better? Does he pay more attention to his children? The rivalry is intense and continuous, and emotions can run on collision courses. The combinations and per-mutations of who's on whose side are endless. Accusations abound! "You don't love me." "You love her more than me." "You always give in to him." Many of these issues are vibrantly present, available for immediate scrutiny and possible resolution. But some of them lurk under the surface, hidden in the deeper waters of resentment and anger. They will occasionally rise up and bear down on the family in a tidal wave of unexpected emotion.

Sometimes feelings are indirectly acted out. He's a good cook, so her children won't eat his food. She loves order, so his children create chaos wherever they can. Everyone brings his or her own feelings to this new family table, each wanting some intangible something to help make the situation better. In the beginning no one knows quite what to do to accomplish that task. In the folklore of group living, "two's company, three's a crowd." In the blended family, the numbers grow from two to six or eight right before our eyes. If "three's a crowd," six or more is nearly a riot!

Insufficient Funds

Much as we might like to minimize the effect of money on our sense of well-being, in fact, lack of money is at the root of many of the problems of any family. Having enough can make a difference, but *not* having enough can create a disaster. In the blended family, money is a very complicated issue. With rare exceptions, most blended families are very short of money. Support payments from a former spouse are rarely sufficient to cover expenses for the children. One parent may still be making support payments to a former spouse. Old debts from either previous marriage can cause anger and resentment and are a reminder of unfinished business persisting into the new family.

Combining expenses does not necessarily mean reducing costs. Many blended families have to move into larger space to accommodate the increased size of the group. Larger housing costs more; food costs more; even at the local fast-food establishment, dinner for eight is a lot more expensive than dinner for two. The distractions we all use to soften the frustrations in life are usually unavailable to the blended family because they cost too much. Setting money aside for future needs such as college may be virtually impossible, and such financial strictures may be deeply painful for parents to acknowledge. There is a continual awareness of the limitations of economic resources.

Along with not having enough money, the blended family has perhaps the more complicated task of deciding who's in charge of what money there is. Whose money goes for what expenses? Is there his money, her money, and our money? Even using democratic principles for guidance, we can get lost in the more pressing challenge of who has the greatest need. What *must* come first? Who can wait? What can we put off? Who has top priority?

Insufficient Time

Along with insufficient money, the blended family faces a major problem of insufficient time. The time required for these blended parents to accomplish all the tasks of caring for the family usually consumes any time they might have for themselves as individuals or as a couple. The demands on their time are so constant and so profound they simply don't have any moments, let alone hours, for intimacy and companionship. In order to provide for everyone else's needs, their own needs must go on hold. There simply isn't time for everything and everyone.

But the price for this loss of time is very high. Without sufficient time for companionship and love, blended marriages enter dangerous waters. When the marital relationship has to be neglected because there are other more pressing needs, the whole family is in jeopardy. If this new family goes aground, everyone faces the legacy of another lost family. It's too high a price to pay.

Partners in a blended marriage have no choice except to find time for themselves. That is as essential to the health of their relationship as food and shelter are to their physical survival. The whole blended family needs this partnership to have a solid center. Such a center cannot be created without the couple spending time together.

In addition, the entire blended family needs time, simply the passing of time, in order to survive all the changes and stresses and build a more solid foundation as a family. At first no one had any idea how much time it would take to solidify a blended family. One year? Two years? Our best guess was vastly underestimated. It is now known that it takes from five to seven years before a blended family begins to look as if it might survive. All kinds of problems still have to be worked out. But if everyone hangs on long enough, the family will probably manage the crises of blending and become connected.

The trouble for many blended marriages is they end too soon, not giving themselves enough time to accomplish what needs to be done. Families can't hold out quite long enough. Pressures mount, problems become overwhelming, and people give up, desperately wishing things were different.

Couples go into a remarriage having already struggled and lost. If another marriage also fails, the injury to each person's self-esteem is profound and long lasting. One feels on the verge of "three strikes and you're out." It's much too close for comfort.

THE POTENTIAL FOR HEALING

The blended family offers both the worst and best of family life. The worst is when everyone vies for attention, and the accumulated needs of each person seem overwhelming and impossible to satisfy; or when the pressures become so great that everyone realizes the family is on the brink of collapse.

The best is when the blended family operates as a healing agent in the immediate present. Issues of the past *can* be worked out because they *are* available in this new situation. Jealousies and other competitive feelings are so blatant they can't be swept under the rug of denial. Money is in short supply; therefore other ways of entertainment and pleasure must be found. Usually this means more opportunity for better verbal communication. There's no place to hide in a blended family, which means there's a good chance to learn cooperative living.

Blended families require a combination of love, devotion, commitment, and hard work to succeed. It takes an incredible amount of love between the remarried partners, who are willing to take on so much, with so little to help them. It takes a great deal of patience and trust on the part of children to endure the experience of living with strangers who've become intimately involved in their lives. It takes a long-range commitment to the unknown future and a willingness to work hard in the present, with little time off. As problems from the past emerge into this new family, they are given the opportunity for healing. But healing can't happen without the risk of honesty and the trust of commitment.

It will take time to create a sense of trust and ease in a remarriage and a blended family. The partners cannot force this creation but must work for it and wait for it to happen. The process will be discouraging and trying; many times it will feel quite hopeless. But occasionally, they will catch a glimpse of the healing that is taking place, they will sense the meaning of all the work and commitment, and they will know it was worth all the effort. Blended families who stay together deserve great credit. Their reward is in their courage and persistence in not giving up. They know the power of family because they've lived it!

STEPPARENTING

A few observations may help promote a better relationship between a stepparent and a stepchild.

It's no good one spouse asking the other to control the behavior of his or her children without the first spouse being willing to be an active participant in the interaction. In other words, stepparenting doesn't mean one parent directing the other parent in ways of child care, from the sidelines. Instead a stepparent must perform an active parental role toward all the children growing up in the home. A stepparent is an integral part of the parenting team. As such, he or she must form a personal relationship with each stepchild. If that relationship is avoided, the opportunity for contact is lost and the family remains divided, much as it was prior to the remarriage.

Stepparents can make a unique contribution to the growth and development of the child. They can offer the advantage of adults who aren't so emotionally involved with the child that their vision is blurred and their judgment impaired. Stepparents can approach the child with dispassion, offering parental suggestions that the child often finds more tolerable because they come from a nonparental source. Stepparents can be a kind of channel for the child's feelings, conveying them in more understandable ways and defending the child's right to have these feelings because stepparents don't have to absorb such feelings themselves.

But stepparents can also be the object of negative, projected feelings from the child, which cut into the family like sharp knives of anger and rejection. No stepparent is exempt from a child's resentment over his or her presence in the family. Like the fairy tales where wicked stepmothers (are there no wicked stepfathers?)

create havoc and disruption, stepparents may be viewed as intruders and interlopers, who need to be banished forever!

When children find they cannot succeed in that wish, they have the chance to break free of overly dependent entanglements with their own parents and form a special kind of friendship with the stepparent who's willing to engage in a personal relationship. Such a friendship can be deeply satisfying and last a lifetime. It's that special kind of relationship a stepparent can offer a child, grown or not, that is the greatest gift of a remarriage and a blended family. Stepparents can see without the cloudiness of emotional investment. They can dispense wisdom without needing approval from the child. They can be honest without needing to be loved. They can listen and not have to be right. They are special adult friends who have a commitment that is uniquely nonemotional and accepting of the child, thereby providing him or her with optimal conditions for growth and development.

Stepparents who do not respect and care about their stepchildren play a dangerous role. Children are remarkably astute in their assessment of how people feel about them. Children in a blended family are particularly vulnerable. They need to experience a consistency of care to recover from the trauma of separation, either from divorce or death.

If a stepparent isn't willing to form a relationship of respect and care, a child is wounded all over again. Children will do their best to hide their feelings of hurt and resentment in order to survive. But their pain and anger will seethe inside, cutting them off from any form of healing or comfort. *A stepparent who is not willing to form a reasonable relationship with stepchildren should not form a blended family.* It's asking too much of children to face an additional source of rejection at such an intimate level. They would have no choice except to withdraw because their feelings become so intense. Ultimately their compressed anger and pain will explode in predictable outbursts that are destructive to the whole family. Stepparents, therefore, must form a special "parental alliance" within the blended family, which guarantees their caring involvement with their stepchildren. The family needs to have this stated commitment as a basic foundation understood by all.

In many ways the stepparent is like an adoptive parent. Many adopted children at some point in their lives need to locate their biological parent in order to discover their origins. Their search reminds us how basic the biological parenting connection really is. Even after giving years of loving care, the adoptive parent, like the stepparent, also faces the reality and challenge of not being a biological parent.

Consequently a fundamental limitation is built into the structure of the blended family. It can offer healing, respite, and a sanctuary of growth. It can provide for basic needs and emotional support. It offers a generous gift of care and love that allows children to proceed toward adulthood. But it also has to face the residues and realities of former family relationships.

Unlike the adoptive parent, who usually remains the core parent, the stepparent must graciously accept the role of secondary parent, regardless of the quality of the relationship with the stepchild. The role is essential and life-giving, but the reward may have to be understood as an expression of the generosity of the giver.

The person who's willing to take on this role reflects the best qualities of humanity: a willingness to care for others without direct reward, a capacity for empathic understanding, and an ability to set aside one's own needs for the greater good. Such a person is rather like a modern-day Good Samaritan with the additional requirements of having to live with the situation rather than leaving it behind.

Because this role is so frequently challenged and unrewarded, it requires great support and understanding on the part of the other partner and a joint awareness of the profound task they've undertaken. In the blending of two families, each parent takes on a double parenting job. The job is to help pick up the pieces of *everyone's* life and help the natural growth process resume, like restoring the neighborhood after a bomb has exploded. It's no surprise that such an effort takes an enormous amount of time and that many remarried couples spend far more hours parenting than doing anything else.

If one of the partners comes into the marriage without children of his or her own, the situation may feel very lopsided. The unequal distribution of emotional energy has the potential to cause deep resentment and disappointment for both partners. The necessary requirements of parenting in blended families can become divisive, threatening the marriage with extinction. The partnership requires the active support and understanding of the extended family for whatever time it takes to solidify and ensure the future of the blended family. But this agenda also restores and revitalizes the concept of the richness of the extended family and validates the connections of care that are the essence of family living.

At no other time in our history have we so much needed these connections. The experience of being part of a network of respect and care, held together by the glue of commitment, seems like an oasis in the middle of the present-day desert of uncaring, isolated, self-absorbed individuals.

The stakes are high in a blended family, but the rewards are life changing. The price is commitment. The goal is an extended family whose members are connected by respect, responsibility, and caring. The blended family stands out as a group of individuals struggling to succeed together. If there's a lesson to be learned from their efforts, it's a lesson of courage in the midst of adversity, trust in the midst of challenge, and love in the midst of change.

17

The Functional Family

The profound and unceasing societal changes of the last sixty years, especially the rising divorce rate, have battered the family and severely shaken our confidence in its permanence. More recently a further blow against the family has been the emphasis on the dysfunctional family. While we are focusing on our inadequate families, we are missing the fact of our dysfunctional American society and the rapid changes and isolating philosophy of narcissism that have helped bring it about.

THE DYSFUNCTIONAL FAMILY

The concept of the dysfunctional family has become the new rallying cry of a society in pain. This current indictment of the family seems to negate the existence of any functional families in our society. The recommended remedy is for individual members to break free of the dysfunctional bonds of the family by becoming involved in a new kind of self-absorption. This renewed emphasis on narcissism further encourages us to become healthy as individuals while maintaining protective boundaries against involvement with others. The idea is that I can do or say anything I want. How other people take it is *their* problem. The necessity for this behavior, and sometimes its rationalization, is that we've come from dysfunctional families and must break free of those unhealthy interferences with our being able to live as whole persons. If it is true that we all come from dysfunctional families, then the problem is catastrophic in scope and there's little hope for the future of the family.

The large numbers of people attracted to this idea are a testimony to our continued desperation and need for healing. In fact, there is a great deal of truth to what is being said. All families *are* dysfunctional at various times. No one could accuse the family of being a perfect institution. No family always operates at high levels of good judgment and appropriate behaviors. No family is exempt from stupidity, lack of awareness, or just plain wrong actions. Individual members are also subject to their own inadequacies and anxieties from the pressures of changes in the family and society. Abusive families are dangerous and destructive. Harmful behaviors should never be tolerated. There's no question about that.

But what has happened is the extension of a concept into a way of life. In fact, the majority of families struggle to function as a family. That is, they attempt to perform the proper functions of a family: to love, protect, educate, and release its members. Even those families with blatant disruptions and upheavals may be continuing to try to function as a family, albeit at levels that are totally inadequate to the task. The family is an extremely complicated entity struggling in a variety of ways to stay afloat in an unstable and changing society. Obstacles and interferences are everywhere. Judging its performance as almost universally dysfunctional is too easy an indictment and often tends to operate as a rationalization for severing any connections to one's original family.

The narcissistic view that supports the focus on the dysfunctional family is an expected outcome of the last thirty years of concentration on the self. We must also recognize that the cult of self-indulgence is economically good for some people. But the cost of our continued narcissism to the emotional health of the nation is devastating. Like the national debt, we don't begin to know the damage done by our unwillingness to deal with this issue. If narcissism is injurious to our relationships with others, it is lethal to the family, the basic structure of society.

Families continue to struggle to be functional in what appears to be a very dysfunctional world. Rather than concentrating on the family as an ongoing dysfunctional influence, we need to look at the ways in which American society has come loose from a structure of authority and discipline, which had guaranteed our freedom rather than interfered with it. Our focus on individual rights rather than responsibilities to others is destroying our chances to be a society where concern for others can exist. By blaming the dysfunctional families of our past and by operating in the present solely for our own gratification, we've effectively canceled our ability to live in the future.

Accompanied by the incessant drumbeat of societal change, we've moved inexorably from a reliable, predictable world into one of profound uncertainty. Nothing is forever; no one is indispensable; everything is disposable. In this "disposable society" we throw away those things we don't need any longer or don't want to be bothered with, from disposable diapers and containers to disposable relationships. We've even created new industries to get rid of a whole variety of disposables.

Families are deeply affected by what happens in society. When society breaks loose from its moorings, families are not far behind. The loss of authority in society is intensified within the family when parents cannot or will not do their job of parenting. The self-absorption fostered by narcissism is expressed in rebellion from the family, shattered family connections, and withdrawal from others into isolation. The theme of disposability in the world around us is extended to families when we indict them as dysfunctional.

Our ability to endure these assaults depends on our willingness to face them as a collective unit, not as individuals standing alone. The family is the most available, healing collective we have. We need to acknowledge its amazing, creative power and resilience as well as recognize its problems and imperfections. We need to celebrate the remarkable ways it does function, rather than focus on its failures.

LACK OF TIME AND LACK OF CONNECTIONS

One of the most important forces undermining families today, as noted earlier, is lack of time. We don't have enough time to form the kinds of relational bonds we need. We substitute goods for time in our attempt to stay together geographically while living apart emotionally. We buy expensive equipment for family entertainment. We hope the cost will make the family feel that it is important to us. But even when we're physically together being entertained, we're inwardly separate and unconnected. Machines can't replace the exchange of feelings and the intimacy of dialogue.

We try to find "quality time" to replace the "quantity time" we used to have. But in seeking a special time we lose the experience of ordinary time, that slow, steady sequence of everyday happenings that binds us together and reassures us of our reliable connections.

As we reduce the amount of ordinary time we spend together, we automatically weaken the family. Families are not built upon the special vacations they take together. They are constructed of hundreds of small interactions that mount up like bricks in a wall, held together by the mortar of responsibility and love. The more everyone participates in the work, the stronger the wall will be. Special events are like decorative cornices and moldings. They enhance the beauty and uniqueness but do not create the basic structure.

Also weakening families today is the loss of the extended family. When we became a mobile society in the 1950s, many of us set out on the road to independence and self-sufficiency. We thought we'd become mature enough to leave the "folks" behind and make our way into new territories. Instead, we discovered how connected we were to a family history that continues to manifest itself, even in our independence. In fact, we're genetically connected to past generations, and we're emotionally connected to the family network that we grew up with. For better or for worse, we're part of a family system of great diversity and complexity.

In the past the extended family included people we loved, people we couldn't stand, people who treated us well, and people who didn't give us the time of day. One person's favorite was someone else's enemy. A friendly relative one day might become an antagonistic one the next day. Relationships in the extended family might shift like the tides, but *they were there*.

Our contacts with the extended family generally are precarious today because of the geographic distances between us and especially the shortage of time. If there's little time for the immediate family, there's virtually no time for the extended family. Relationships die for want of attention. People seem to disappear; the family shrinks. Only at holidays and special family occasions are we aware of what we've lost. Weddings remind us of our strength in numbers. Look at how many of us came to celebrate this new family. Funerals remind us of what we've tried to forget. Time passes and no one is permanent. Look at what we've missed by living so separately.

Very often our neighborhood "family" has suffered a similar decline. Many front porches where we used to sit and chat about happenings in the neighborhood have been replaced by individual units in high-rise apartment houses, where no one gets together except in meetings to discuss policy. Many neighborhoods that used to be noisy and full of the traffic of daily life are now deserted in the daytime; empty houses wait passively for their occupants to return at night after work, turn on the lights, and resume the business of living. We've become isolated householders, guarding our territory against the unknown forces around us.

THE STRENGTHS OF THE FUNCTIONAL FAMILY

If we are to reverse the forces operating against the family, we must focus on the strengths of those families who *are* trying to function as care givers and protectors of the young.

The Marital Couple

We know that the pivotal relationship in the family has been the marital partnership. When that is going well, the rest of the family are able to go about their business of growing, learning, and leaving the premises. When the marital relationship is strained, the entire family is interrupted. If the conflict ends in divorce, the family is fractured and needs repair and healing.

The reality of divorce has not diminished the importance of the marital relationship, even when it is terminated. The survival of the family after a divorce depends on continuing good will between former married partners. The parental alliance previously discussed allows couples to continue their obligations to their children, providing them with an ongoing set of responsible parents. Couples who cannot provide this stability themselves must find other persons to stand in for the missing partner, either through remarriage or contracting with a willing participant. We now understand how essential it is that children have two parenting persons to meet their needs. The ways we provide for that parenting function are changing. But the picture remains the same. Without proper parenting, children cannot grow into well-functioning adults.

Grandparents and the Extended Family

Second only in importance to the marital couple, or a parent and a stand-in, are the grandparents of the family. There's no relationship in the world like that between grandparents and grandchildren. It skips over unfinished business from the middle generation, transcends the duty of parenting (except in circumstances where parenting is required), and offers the gifts of pure acceptance and love.

The connection between the old and the young, those who are ending their lives and those who are beginning theirs, completes one life cycle and begins another. The generations are linked in a never ending cycle of creation and passing away. The old give the young their attention and love; the young give the old a sense of value and meaning as well as affection. The exchange takes place within the most ordinary circumstances of life.

Once we broke loose from our extended family connections, we simply lost this gift of grandparents. Many of us no longer live near our parents, and therefore our children do not experience unlimited time with their grandparents. Instead we visit each other and frantically try to create normal interactions within a miniature time frame. Once, perhaps twice a year we congregate to be a family only to rediscover our separateness. There's simply too much territory between us. Acknowledging the need for contact between grandparents and grandchildren highlights the gifts each have for the other, which are unstructured time and faithful love.

One of the remarkable realities about families is the thread of connection that runs from one generation to the next. The repetition of physical characteristics is obvious. She looks just like her grandmother. He is the image of his father. Everyone in the family has that same high forehead. Additional connections are just beginning to be acknowledged. Tendencies toward addictive behavior crop up in one generation after another. A family secret such as incest is often carried into the next generation. Genetic predispositions toward physical and emotional illness weave in and out of the family. We're connected at far deeper levels than we have realized and we need to know these connections to utilize their information.

One of the unexpected losses in a divorce is the close relationship between grandparents and grandchildren. A divorce settlement provides for time for parents to spend with their children, but it does not usually include time for grandparents. They may slip through the cracks of the dissolution unless a special effort is made to allocate time for them.

Grandparents are not usually anxious to be caught in the divorce fray. They stand on the sidelines, hoping to continue their contact with their grandchildren so that they can offer some kind of stability and protection. But they're often caught in the conflict, especially if it continues to be bitter and hateful. When resolution finally occurs, their relationship to their grandchildren may be utterly changed unless both sides are willing to acknowledge the essential nature of that relationship and the need for sufficient time together.

One of the modern-day, postdivorce miracles occurs when the first grandchild arrives after a divorce. This child, who belongs to *all* parts of the family, represents the beginning of a new generation and the possibility of healing in the family. We can be reunited around this special gift. Animosities can disappear in the very presence of a baby. Resentments can be at least temporarily set aside in the miraculous offering of a new life. We are not completely separated from each other because we are participating in a new beginning. What we thought was destroyed has entered a new phase. The family continues.

The benefits offered by the extended family are part of the functionality of the family, and we're emotionally impoverished when we cut ourselves off from that interlocking network of support. No matter how insufficient or inadequate that extended family may be, its numbers and connections are its potential strength.

We see the fullness of the loss of the extended family when we look at the numbers of self-help groups that have emerged to try to take that place in our lives. People are constantly showing us what they're missing by their hunger for familial experiences of almost any kind. If there was ever an endorsement for the family, it's surely seen in the emptiness people feel without it and the need they have to find a replacement.

THE NEED FOR THE FUNCTIONAL FAMILY

As new family forms have come into being, nothing has yet changed our perception of the functionality of families. Single-parent families struggle in terribly deprived circumstances but are no less a family for their hardships. Blended families, in spite of their high failure rate, are trying to provide sanctuary and healing for family members. The parental alliance is a creative response to the need for continued parenting. Even children in so-called dysfunctional families who are being disruptive and disagreeable may be attempting to draw attention to themselves in order to keep the family together. We've not given up on family life. Nothing in the foreseeable future indicates we will.

The functioning of the family is an essential protection for our future. It was postulated earlier in this book that the societal changes of the last sixty years, and the resulting changes in the family, have created two major, but interrelated problems: the breakdown of the functioning family and a critical loss of parenting.

We are now able to see the long-range effect of these changes in society and in the family as they have affected the lives of children. The product of insufficient parenting and a breakdown in the functioning family is a child who is wounded and angry, a child who cannot grow into his or her full potential, a child who may retaliate against those who have denied her or him a chance for normal development.

We cannot treat children as if there were no limits to what they can tolerate. They are not miniature adults. Their vulnerability demands our responsible care. If we are not willing to assume responsibility for their well-being, while they are dependent on us for care and protection, we need to ask ourselves why we are having them in the first place.

The danger to our children is increasing at a frightening rate. Information released from the Commission on Adolescent Development in June 1990 described American adolescents as not physically or emotionally prepared for adulthood. Their drug and alcohol consumption is increasing as well as their suicide rate. In fact, the most frequent cause of death among adolescents is now suicide. Surely the message could not be clearer. Many children are growing unwilling and unable to survive in American society. They lack the emotional well-being to become adults; they seem more interested in distracting themselves with illegal substances than in facing the emptiness and fear within. The present holds too little attraction; the future is too frightening to contemplate. Too many of these children have lost hope.

Part of their hopelessness comes from our lack of care for them. If they're not important enough for us to care about them, why should they bother looking after themselves? If we don't see fit to make a commitment to them, why should they commit themselves to any constructive future? Our consuming self-interest is partly to blame. Why should they trust in society when the basic unit of society, the family, does not provide for their needs?

Their despair may also be deeply connected to our despair. When we find life to be without meaning and hope, we transfer a message to our children that life isn't worth struggling for. If we're to have a future generation that will guide and protect our society, we have no choice but to care for our children now. The functional family is our best and perhaps only hope of doing so. The question is how seriously we will take the information we have. What more has to happen to convince us of the urgency of the situation. What will it take before we decide to take action on behalf of the family?

18

Where Do We Go from Here?

In the last sixty years we've undergone a revolution in our family life that has taken us on an orbit of change. We've journeyed through various constellations of family types, while being bombarded by profound changes and the frightening challenges they present. This book has raised four areas of deep concern to the family: (1) the loss of parenting, (2) the dissolution of the immediate family and the extended family, (3) significant changes in the developmental life cycle of the individual, and (4) profound changes in the moral values of society. How we deal with these concerns will determine the future for all of us.

THE LOSS OF PARENTING

The loss of parenting began very quietly when the Depression necessitated the entry of many women into the workplace, as has been noted. It continued through the wartime economy of the 1940s and accelerated and changed direction in the 1950s, when we began to blur the boundaries between parents and children. At that time we didn't realize that parents have to stay in their role as parents so that children can be protected as children.

Our dream of the equality of generations was shattered in the

1960s when parent-child relationships were strained almost to the breaking point. We began to lose confidence as parents and became less and less able to set limits on our children's behavior. As the tempo of change increased in the 1970s and 1980s, we reached the limit of our capacity to withstand the challenges of adolescent children, who promptly took charge. Ironically, although they demanded their independence, they needed us to stand firm in our parental positions. We misread their signals and effectively gave up our role as parents. More and more adolescents responded by deciding not to grow up.

In the meantime, more women entered the job market, creating the need for day-care centers and baby-sitters. A rising divorce rate and an increasing number of unwed mothers created single-parent families, which also needed child care, sometimes for infants as young as two or three weeks of age.

The result has been that too many children are not being adequately parented. We've created a population of children who are profoundly deficient in their development. Without the foundation of adequate parental care, many of these children will never live fulfilled lives as responsible members of the adult community.

THE DISSOLUTION OF THE FAMILY

The dissolution of the family began after the war, in the 1950s, when people began to move to different parts of the country to take advantage of new economic opportunities. The nuclear family was on its own, cut off from the support, care, and traditions of the extended family network.

Dissolution continued in the 1960s, when divorce began increasingly to break apart the nuclear family. As husband and wife separated and set up separate households, whoever remained of the extended family often found it difficult to establish relationships with both former spouses, further cutting off extended-family connections. Later, as undisciplined, rebellious children challenged parental authority and there were no extended-family members to mediate, the risk of family dissolution increased. As adolescents carried these challenges to schools and other authorities, a disrupted society seemed to be moving toward anarchy. The dissolution of the family was further encouraged by the narcissism that emphasized individual fulfillment at the expense of the family and society.

New family forms desperately tried to maintain the structure of the family, against almost impossible odds. The single parent faced overwhelming responsibilities in the task of raising children alone. The remarried couple in a blended family struggled to restore some sense of family in an emotionally chaotic environment. Too often each of these families has been alone in their struggle. Society doesn't offer direct assistance so that weary parents can have some time off. And it doesn't offer them the kind of meaningful understanding and support that would assist them in their attempts to provide a family for their children.

The loss of the extended family has made all of our family life situations more difficult. The network of help that used to be found in the extended family was an essential part of our ability to provide adequate care and protection for children. It provided the reassurance that children must know that they *will* be taken care of, no matter what circumstances arise in the family. Today children have no such guarantees that they will be cared for and protected.

CHANGES IN THE DEVELOPMENTAL LIFE CYCLE

We have hurried our young children and latency-age children too quickly through their developmental years, thereby not providing them with the building blocks they need for adequate growth.

Our adolescents have reflected the most significant changes in the life cycle. Having been moved forward too quickly, many teenagers respond by going into slow motion in their move from adolescence into adulthood. The boundary between adolescence and adulthood has become elasticized, stretching and bouncing back in the ambivalence children feel about growing up. In trying to have it both ways—taking a revolving-door kind of approach—many adolescents move into the role of adults as far as privileges and freedoms are concerned but stubbornly retain an adolescent focus on their narcissistic pleasures. Indulgence in drugs, alcohol, and sex convinces them of their grown-up status and temporarily relieves their guilt, but the spector of adult responsibility remains an ever present reminder of what they are not doing with their lives.

Some of them make a successful shift into adulthood. Others try it and return home to stay for an indefinite period of time. Others never move at all. Many remain trapped in their transitional pain, unable to leave their ambivalence and insecurity about growing up.

Society cannot survive if the development stages of the human life cycle are so skewed and abbreviated that future generations refuse to take on adult responsibilities.

CHANGES IN THE MORAL VALUES OF SOCIETY

Traditionally American society has honored such basic values as care, responsibility, integrity, justice, and freedom. But we have distorted our love for freedom and transformed it into narcissistic license to do or say whatever we want, without regard for anyone else. The Bill of Rights has become a statement of demands. Constitutional guarantees of life, liberty, and the pursuit of happiness have been corrupted into a me-first, it's-your-problem, get-off-my-back attitude. No one seems to be in charge; rules are a thing of the past; regulated behaviors are regarded as an infringement on "my rights." Social graces are generally regarded as hopelessly outdated; politeness is seen as weakness. The moral code has been diluted into nonexistence. Our ability to distinguish right from wrong tends to dissolve into an outlook that says "anything goes." Our responsibility to others is lost in our preoccupation with "what's in it for me?" We struggle with a painful double message: you're free to do whatever you want versus the ancient admonition to do unto others what you would have them do unto you. Growing into adulthood, being a parent, living in a family, all require the ability to respond to the needs of others. Whether one is a parent or not, recognizing the existence of right and wrong is a requirement of living in a society.

ADDRESSING THE CONCERNS

The journey we have taken has moved us far from the essential values of our humanity. In the process we became fixed in a position that elevated the individual and denied the importance of the family and society. The danger we face now is the very real possibility that we may not find our way back to the fundamental rules of society from which we started.

The function of the family has always been to care for its children. This is not a choice but a mandate. We are in a crisis situation where children are concerned. Our highest priority has to be the planning and implementing of ways to increase the time parents or parenting persons are able to spend with children. Without this intervention, the stage is set for a future society of adult children incapable of taking on adult responsibilities. Because we know what children need for their growth and development, we can no longer ignore their plight. Each of us spends some time with children, either our own or others. We can be aware of their needs for contact with an adult person who can demonstrate what caring, responsible adults are like. Some of us have access to policy making as it pertains to the welfare of children, through business, school, church, or community. We don't have the right to destroy their future through our inaction. Ultimately it will be our future that is destroyed as well.

The family in all its diversity is still the most important unit in society for providing for the health and well-being of everyone. We need to recover our sense of healthy cohesion in a multigenerational family with differences but with a common goal: the care and maintenance of its members. But instead of finding ways to affirm and support family life, we denigrate it or deny its importance. We've lost both the creative power of the extended family and the connections of the immediate family as we have become isolated individuals absorbed in self-concerns.

Surely, we can address that problem through a renewed attempt to rebuild the extended family network. We might also work toward the renewal of the neighborhood family, particularly as an immediate caring network in times of emergency. The religious institution, carrying the label of God's family, offers each of us an essential identity in a world in which we feel disconnected and alone. Through our families and our extended families of all kinds, we have the means to innoculate ourselves against the narcissism that has been so injurious to our society. It is a sickness we must erradicate.

Adulthood is not the valued position it used to be. If it were, there would not be so much anger, frustration, and despair and so many schemes to make people feel better about their lives. The definition of a good life as one of economic success has put great strains on the family by demanding time previously given to family intimacy. Too many adults are overburdened by responsibilities and underfed in their needs for companionship and care. "Is this all there is to life?" is the question they raise when life seems hopelessly out of balance. Most adults feel quite helpless to alter the situation because society itself feels so changed. The anger and rage around us is palpable. One of the most vivid symbols for our current emotional state is "the finger" that is raised so freely in traffic situations. The gesture says, "How dare you get in my way?" or "I don't give a damn about you." Our response is often to return anger for anger, a spontaneous, immediate reaction out of our own sense of rage and frustration. Like some animal who's been attacked, we counterattack and are caught in a life or death struggle—over traffic. In the immediacy of the moment, our reactive buttons have been pushed. But in the exchange, our humanity is lost.

It is ironic to feel such inner pain and helplessness in a world that has become so successfully mechanized. Our communication systems are expressions of creative genius. Through television we can "see" the rest of the world and its needs. We're beginning to think responsibly about this planet and the ways we are destroying it. We're exploring the space beyond the planet, evidence of our ability to work together on a task and bring it to completion. We've made major strides in health care and are on the edge of understanding the genetic structure of life.

Yet all these technological successes only make our human pain feel worse. For it is the very gift of life that seems to be in so much jeopardy. We've lost the sense of the preciousness of the gift, regarding life as something to be endured, not treasured. When we do not treasure and care for it, life becomes tarnished and corrupted. It loses its enduring qualities and becomes diseased and we become life-less, separated from other lives and alone. Surely our current preoccupation with television soap operas and romance novels is final proof of our desperate longing for that which will distract us or make us feel better.

In times of great change, basic truths become evident if we are willing to see them. Our sixty years of change have reminded us of what happens when we break off our family connections, stop parenting, seek to satisfy ourselves at the expense of others, eliminate the rules and morals of society, and cease to value the miracle of life.

We were created to live in harmony with one another. We are fundamentally and irrevocably connected to one another. Life becomes a personal and collective disaster when we operate against the basic truths of our existence.

▷ When we cease to parent our children properly, we destroy the present and cut ourselves off from the future.

▷ When we disconnect from our family heritage, we lose the wisdom of the past.

▷ When we operate out of a narcissistic center, we deny our common humanity and lose the opportunity to care for others and be cared for by them.

▷ When we deny the existence of rules of behavior and blur the difference between right and wrong, we eliminate justice, freedom, and safety from our lives.

▷ When we devalue the miracle of life with cynicism and negativity, we are severed from our spiritual center.

▷ When we lose our spiritual center, we lose all sense of meaning and direction in life.

Over the last sixty years, we have lost both our sense of direction and our belief that life has ultimate meaning and purpose. The secular society we live in has been increasingly ineffective in providing any rules and guidelines to help us. It has become particularly unable to help us distinguish between right and wrong actions. The traps of narcissism and permissiveness keep us too disconnected to be actively concerned for the welfare of others. Everything seems to be shifting. What we could count on today, is gone tomorrow. What works now may be obsolete next year. We have struggled in vain to find something, anything, that would provide answers to our questions, relief for our pain, and constancy in our lives.

Yet this very ineffectiveness of our secular society now offers religious institutions an incredible opportunity to step into the void created by these changing moral values. Religious values *can* give us a code of behavior toward others, a code society now seems unable to provide. In fact our best hope for survival may be in the firm stance that organized religions *can* take in relation to the preservation of some kind of moral code to guide and direct us.

The particular value of religious teaching to the family is twofold. First, it provides a moral underpinning for ethical behavior and a scheme of ethical actions. Second, it provides a community of people who are attempting to practice this behavior and follow these moral principles, thus reinforcing the behaviors the family needs to teach.

This present chaotic situation may present an unexpected opportunity for the renewal of spiritual values and the development of our spiritual life. As the emptiness of self-involvement has become painfully evident and as the disconnection from our families has increased, we have become alienated and alone. We need a spiritual connection that will allow us to redirect our attention and energy away from ourselves toward the community of others where we can find a renewed sense of meaning and purpose to our lives.

Finally it remains for us to acknowledge what we've learned, gather our collective forces, and make a plan of action. All of us bear responsibility for our participation in these years we've just survived, but no single effort in the work of transformation will go unnoticed. We are part of the problem, but we are also an essential part of the solution. Each one of us, without exception, is called to the task at hand.

If the task seems overwhelming, if one person's contributions seem insignificant or unworthy, the wisdom of systems theory can help us direct our efforts. To introduce stability into any complex system, we need only to start with *one* change as the initiator of the action we seek. Other changes will follow in due course. What that means is that it takes only one move to create a domino effect. A single step taken by each of us can cause a chain reaction of change. We don't have to accomplish the entire task. We have only to choose the proper starting place.

Our beginning must take place at the start of the life cycle, with a commitment to our children, the most innocent and vulnerable members of our society. It is their fundamental right to be cared for until they can care for themselves. It is our responsibility to provide that care.

Throughout its pages, this book has drawn the visible connection between historical events and changes in family life. We've seen history operate as a predictor of things to come, so that we can frequently anticipate cause and effect. Once again, we have the chance to change history. We have a responsibility to the future we can no longer ignore. The actions we take now will sound their influence for generations to come.

Let us therefore commit ourselves to a new course of action, guided by what we have learned, and with the understanding of the urgency of our task. With our chosen starting place, the problems we've described will finally be addressed.

19

Questions for Reflection

There are no easy answers to the complex problems presented in this book. Rather than offer quick solutions that do not work, it seems more helpful to raise questions that will start discussion and lead toward resolution.

1. There's been a growing assumption in American society that one's primary responsibility is to oneself. Unfortunately this narcissistic view runs counter to the needs of children for parental care and sufficient time devoted to their growth and development. In the light of the current family crisis, what new images of the self do we need to construct in order to ensure that children are properly parented and able to reach responsible adulthood?

2. It has been commonly assumed that if parents just actively loved their children, the children would turn out fine. In point of fact, parents have to provide boundaries, structure, discipline, protection, and a lot of information about living as well as love. These tasks take a considerable amount of time spent directly with children if they are to be accomplished. How can we reorganize our priorities so that we can spend this kind of time with our children?

3. Many people have assumed that the school system, as well as educating children, is able to provide a wide variety of parenting functions that are not being provided in the home. It is clear,

however, that if teachers have both to parent and counsel their students, the time available for teaching will be shortchanged. How can we return the schools to their proper educational function?

4. It has generally been assumed that given its resources and expertise, the government can provide solutions for family problems more effectively than private citizens can. But the record shows that governmental solutions address symptoms, not their causes. How can we reintroduce responsible parenting without government involvement?

5. It is a widespread assumption today that concepts of right and wrong are relative. This assumption makes it impossible to evaluate and distinguish between courses of action and various lifestyles. How can we return to a moral standard that does not become oppressive but that mandates evaluative decisions?

6. An assumption promoted by various popular psychologies is that eliminating guilt feelings will make people happy. It's a variation on the narcissistic theme of seeking only one's own pleasure and doing whatever one wants. In fact, feeling guilty is an appropriate response to a whole range of situations, and it requires us to change our behavior in certain circumstances. How can we paint a new picture of what it means to be an adult that includes experiences of both pleasure and pain?

7. Another popular assumption is that working hard and striving for excellence are not only unnecessary but a foolish waste of time. For many people this thinking permeates their view of home, school, and the job. How do we reintroduce a realistic work ethic that is not colored by narcissism?

8. The mobility of American society and its narcissistic preoccupations have seriously damaged the extended family. What can we do to reunite it, especially in situations of divorce, remarriage, and single-parent families?

9. Many older people are relegated to a low status in American society and suffer a deteriorating quality of life. Too many people fail to recognize that most of us will be old one day, and generally it is only old people who have acquired the wisdom of life to give to the rest of us. How can we redefine the place of old people in a society that has such a fixation on youth?

10. Many people assume that it takes two incomes for a family to live. Is that true for all economic levels? What measuring standards are we using?

11. Many communities have single-parent families where the children need another parent figure. As a solution for a child in need, would you be willing to be a co-parent in a parental alliance, presuming there were no legal ties or financial obligations? Why or why not?

12. Many people feel powerless as individuals in the face of the great social upheavals of the last sixty years. But it is individuals who contribute to these changes, and each of us is one of those individuals. We have the same power today that individuals have always had to say, "This is where I draw the line." What action will *you* take to ensure the future of the family?

SUGGESTED READING

Growth and Development

Baruch, Dorothy. *One Little Boy.* New York: Dell Publishing Co., 1964.

English, O. Spurgeon, and Gerald H. J. Pearson. *Emotional Problems of Living.* New York: W. W. Norton & Co., 1963.

Fraiberg, Selma. *The Magic Years.* New York: Charles Scribner's Sons, 1959.

Hoopes, Margaret, and James Harper. *Birth Order Roles and Sibling Patterns in Individual and Family Therapy.* Rockville, Md.: Aspen Publishers, 1987.

Kaplan, Louise. *Adolescence: The Farewell to Childhood.* New Jersey: Jason Aronson, 1986.

Kaplan, Louise. *Oneness and Separateness: From Infant to Individual.* New York: Simon & Schuster, 1978.

Miller, Alice. *Prisoners of Childhood.* New York: Basic Books, 1981.

Napier, Augustus, with Carl Whitaker. *The Family Crucible.* New York: Bantam Books, 1980.

Marriage and Divorce

Hendrix, Harville. *Getting the Love You Want.* New York: Henry Holt Co., 1988.

Scarf, Maggie. *Intimate Partners. Patterns in Love and Marriage.* New York: Random House, 1987.

Wallerstein, Judith, and Sandra Blakeslee. *Second Chances*. New York: Ticknor & Fields, 1989.

Wallerstein, Judith, and Joan Kelly. *Surviving the Breakup*. New York: Basic Books, 1980.

Women and Men

"The American Man: 1946–1986." *Esquire*, June, 1986.

Bly, Robert. *Iron John: A Book About Men*. Reading, Mass.: Addison Wesley, 1990.

Gilligan, Carol. *In a Different Voice*. Cambridge, Mass.: Harvard University Press, 1982.

Levinson, Daniel. *The Seasons of a Man's Life*. New York: Ballantine Books, 1978.

McKay, Bobbie. *The Unabridged Woman: A Guide to Growing Up Female*. New York: The Pilgrim Press, 1979.

Scarf, Maggie. *Intimate Partners. Patterns in Love and Marriage*. New York: Random House, 1987.

Schaef, Anne Wilson. *Women's Reality*. Minneapolis: Winston Press, 1981.

Tannen, Deborah. *You Just Don't Understand*. New York: William Morrow & Co., 1990.

Psychology

Basch, Michael Franz. *Doing Psychotherapy*. New York: Basic Books, 1980.

Bass, Ellen, and Laura Davis. *The Courage to Heal*. New York: Harper & Row Publishers, 1988.

Castillejo, Irene Claremont de. *Knowing Woman*. New York: Harper & Row Publishers, 1973.

Cherlin, Andrew. *The New American Grandparent*. New York: Basic Books, 1986.

Edinger, Edward. *Ego and Archetype*. New York: Penguin Books, 1972.

Freud, Anna. *Psychoanalysis for Teachers and Parents*. Boston: Beacon Press, 1935.

Gould, Roger. *Transformations: Growth and Change in Adult Life*. New York: Simon & Schuster, 1978.

Kopp, Sheldon. *An End to Innocence*. New York: Macmillan Publishing Co., 1978.

Lerner, Harriet Goldhor. *The Dance of Anger*. New York: Harper & Row Publishers, 1985.

Miller, Jean Baker. *Toward a New Psychology of Women*. Boston: Beacon Press, 1976.

Rubin, Theodore Isaac. *Compassion and Self Hate*. New York: David McKay Co., 1975.

Satir, Virginia. *Peoplemaking*. Palo Alto, Calif.: Science and Behavior Books, 1972.

Storr, Anthony. *The Integrity of Personality*. Middlesex, England: Penguin Books, 1960.

Viorst, Judith. *Necessary Losses*. New York: Simon & Schuster, 1986.

Viscott, David. *The Language of Feelings*. New York: Arbor House, 1976.

Yalom, Irvin D. *Love's Executioner and Other Tales of Psychotherapy*. New York: Basic Books, 1989.

Philosophy and Religion

Erikson, Erik. *Childhood and Society*. New York: W. W. Norton & Co., 1963.

Erikson, Erik. *Insight and Responsibility*. New York: W. W. Norton & Co., 1964.

Frankl, Viktor. *The Unheard Cry for Meaning*. New York: Simon & Schuster, 1978.

Friedman, Edwin. *Generation to Generation*. New York: Guilford Press, 1985.

Fromm, Erich. *The Forgotten Language*. New York: Grove Press, 1951.

Kopp, Sheldon. *If You Meet the Buddha on the Road, Kill Him*. New York: Bantam Books, 1976.

May, Gerald. *Will and Spirit*. San Francisco: Harper & Row Publishers, 1982.

May, Rollo. *Man's Search for Himself*. New York: Signet Books, 1953.

Merton, Thomas. *No Man Is an Island*. New York: Harcourt Brace Jovanovich, 1955.

Peck, M. Scott. *The Road Less Traveled*. New York: Simon & Schuster, 1978.

Nouwen, Henri J. M. *Reaching Out*. Garden City, N.Y.: Doubleday & Co., 1975.

Tillich, Paul. *Love, Power and Justice*. New York: Oxford University Press, 1960.

Tillich, Paul. *The New Being*. New York: Charles Scribner's Sons, 1955.

Health

Alcoholics Anonymous, 3rd. ed. Alcoholics Anonymous World Services, 1976.

Benson, Herbert. *The Relaxation Response*. New York: William Morrow & Co., 1975.

Cousins, Norman. *Head First: The Biology of Hope*. New York: E. P. Dutton, 1989.

Lynch, James. *The Broken Heart: The Medical Consequences of Loneliness*. New York: Basic Books, 1977.

Peele, Stanton. *The Meaning of Addiction*. Lexington, Mass.: Lexington Books, 1985.

Shaffer, Martin. *Life After Stress*. New York: Plenum Press, 1982.

DATE DUE

JE 26 '92	DE 18 '98		
JY 27 '92	DE 17 '99		
AP 26 '94			
OC 13 '94			
NO 15 '94			
DE 13 '94			
OC 20 '95			
NO 25 '95			
NO 2 '96			
DE 05 '96			
MY 29 '98			
OC 12 '99			